MznLnx

Missing Links Exam Preps

Exam Prep for

Modern Advanced Accounting

Larsen, 10th Edition

The MznLnx Exam Prep is your link from the texbook and lecture to your exams.
The MznLnx Exam Preps are unauthorized and comprehensive reviews of your textbooks.

All material provided by MznLnx and Rico Publications (c) 2010
Textbook publishers and textbook authors do not particpate in or contribute to these reviews.

MznLnx

Rico
Publications

Exam Prep for Modern Advanced Accounting
10th Edition
Larsen

Publisher: Raymond Houge
Assistant Editor: Michael Rouger
Text and Cover Designer: Lisa Buckner
Marketing Manager: Sara Swagger
Project Manager, Editorial Production: Jerry Emerson
Art Director: Vernon Lowerui

Product Manager: Dave Mason
Editorial Assitant: Rachel Guzmanji
Pedagogy: Debra Long
Cover Image: Jim Reed/Getty Images
Text and Cover Printer: City Printing, Inc.
Compositor: Media Mix, Inc.

(c) 2010 Rico Publications
ALL RIGHTS RESERVED. No part of this work covered by the copyright may be reproduced or used in any form or by an means--graphic, electronic, or mechanical, including photocopying, recording, taping, Web distribution, information storage, and retrieval systems, or in any other manner--without the written permission of the publisher.

For more information about our products, contact us at:
Dave.Mason@RicoPublications.com

For permission to use material from this text or product, submit a request online to:
Dave.Mason@RicoPublications.com

Printed in the United States
ISBN:

Contents

CHAPTER 1
Ethical Issues in Advanced Accounting — 1

CHAPTER 2
Partnerships: Organization and Operation — 7

CHAPTER 3
Partnership Liquidation and Incorporation; Joint Ventures — 14

CHAPTER 4
Accounting for Branches; Combined Financial Statements — 21

CHAPTER 5
Business Combinations — 24

CHAPTER 6
Consolidated Financial Statements: On Date of Business Combination — 28

CHAPTER 7
Consolidated Financial Statements: Subsequent to Date of Business Combination — 33

CHAPTER 8
Consolidated Financial Statements: Intercompany Transactions — 35

CHAPTER 9
Consolidated Financial Statements: Income Taxes, Cash Flows, Acquisitions — 39

CHAPTER 10
Consolidated Financial Statements: Special Problems — 44

CHAPTER 11
International Accounting Standards; Accounting for Foreign Currency Transactions — 48

CHAPTER 12
Translation of Foreign Currency Financial Statements — 57

CHAPTER 13
Reporting for Components; Interim Reports; Reporting for the SEC — 62

CHAPTER 14
Bankruptcy: Liquidation and Reorganization — 71

CHAPTER 15
Estates and Trusts — 76

CHAPTER 16
Nonprofit Organizations — 77

CHAPTER 17
Governmental Entities: General Fund — 81

CHAPTER 18
Governmental Entities: Other Governmental Funds and Account Groups — 85

CHAPTER 19
Governmental Entities: Proprietary Funds, Fiduciary Funds, Annual Report — 90

ANSWER KEY — 93

TO THE STUDENT

COMPREHENSIVE

The *MznLnx* Exam Prep series is designed to help you pass your exams. Editors at MznLnx review your textbooks and then prepare these practice exams to help you master the textbook material. Unlike study guides, workbooks, and practice tests provided by the texbook publisher and textbook authors, *MznLnx* gives you **all** of the material in each chapter in exam form, not just samples, so you can be sure to nail your exam.

MECHANICAL

The MznLnx Exam Prep series creates exams that will help you learn the subject matter as well as test you on your understanding. Each question is designed to help you master the concept. Just working through the exams, you gain an understanding of the subject--its a simple mechanical process that produces success.

INTEGRATED STUDY GUIDE AND REVIEW

MznLnx is not just a set of exams designed to test you, its also a comprehensive review of the subject content. Each exam question is also a review of the concept, making sure that you will get the answer correct without having to go to other sources of material. You learn as you go! Its the easiest way to pass an exam.

HUMOR

Studying can be tedious and dry. MznLnx's instructional design includes moderate humor within the exam questions on occassion, to break the tedium and revitalize the brain

Chapter 1. Ethical Issues in Advanced Accounting 1

1. The term _____ usually refers to a company that is permitted to offer its registered securities (stock, bonds, etc.) for sale to the general public, typically through a stock exchange, or occasionally a company whose stock is traded over the counter (OTC) via market makers who use non-exchange quotation services.

The term '_____' may also refer to a company owned by the government.

  a. Governmental Accounting Standards Board
  b. Professional association
  c. MicroStrategy
  d. Public Company

2. The _____ (sometimes called 'Peekaboo') is a private-sector, non-profit corporation created by the Sarbanes-Oxley Act, a 2002 United States federal law, to oversee the auditors of public companies. Its stated purpose is to 'protect the interests of investors and further the public interest in the preparation of informative, fair, and independent audit reports'. Although a private entity, the _____ has many government-like regulatory functions, making it in some ways similar to the private Self Regulatory Organizations (SROs) that regulate stock markets and other aspects of the financial markets in the United States.
  a. 3M Company
  b. Financial Crimes Enforcement Network
  c. Public Company Accounting Oversight Board
  d. Pension Benefit Guaranty Corporation

3. _____ is the business practice where a company or a a sales force within a company, inflates its sales figures by forcing more products through a distribution channel than the channel is capable of selling to the world at large. Also known as 'trade loading', this can be the result of a company attempting to inflate its sales figures. Alternatively, it can be a consequence of a poorly managed sales force attempting to meet short term objectives and quotas in a way that is detrimental to the company in the long term.
  a. Consolidated financial statements
  b. Price variance
  c. Refunding
  d. Channel stuffing

4. _____ are financial statements that factor the holding company's subsidiaries into its aggregated accounting figure. It is a representation of how the holding company is doing as a group. The consolidated accounts should provide a true and fair view of the financial and operating conditions of the group.
  a. Replacement cost
  b. Committee on Accounting Procedure
  c. Redemption value
  d. Consolidated financial statements

Chapter 1. Ethical Issues in Advanced Accounting

5. The _____ is a private, not-for-profit organization whose primary purpose is to develop generally accepted accounting principles (GAAP) within the United States in the public's interest. The Securities and Exchange Commission (SEC) designated the _____ as the organization responsible for setting accounting standards for public companies in the U.S. It was created in 1973, replacing the Accounting Principles Board and the Committee on Accounting Procedure of the American Institute of Certified Public Accountants. The _____'s mission is 'to establish and improve standards of financial accounting and reporting for the guidance and education of the public, including issuers, auditors, and users of financial information.'

The _____ is not a governmental body.

   a. Fannie Mae
   b. Public company
   c. Governmental Accounting Standards Board
   d. Financial Accounting Standards Board

6. _____ are journal entries made at the end of an accounting period to transfer temporary accounts to permanent accounts. An 'income summary' account may be used to show the balance between revenue and expenses, or they could be directly closed against retained earnings where dividend payments will be deducted from. This process is used to reset the balance of these temporary accounts to zero for the next accounting period.
   a. Trial balance
   b. Closing entries
   c. Treasury stock
   d. FIFO and LIFO accounting

7. In monetary economics _____ can refer either to a particular _____, for example British Pounds or United States Dollars, or, to the coins and banknotes of a particular _____, which actually form only a small part of the monetary base of a nation's money supply. The other part of a nation's money supply consists of money deposited in banks (sometimes called deposit money), ownership of which can be transferred by means of checks (cheques in the United Kingdom and Australia) or other forms of money transfer such as credit and debit cards. Deposit money and _____ are 'money' in the sense that both are acceptable as a means of exchange, but money need not necessarily be '_____'.
   a. BMC Software, Inc.
   b. 3M Company
   c. BNSF Railway
   d. Currency

8. _____ are formal records of a business' financial activities.

In British English, including United Kingdom company law, _____ are often referred to as accounts, although the term _____ is also used, particularly by accountants.

_____ provide an overview of a business' financial condition in both short and long term.

   a. Notes to the financial statements
   b. Financial statements
   c. 3M Company
   d. Statement of retained earnings

9. The _____ is the national, professional association of CPAs in the United States, with more than 330,000 members, including CPAs in business and industry, public practice, government, and education; student affiliates; and international associates. It sets ethical standards for the profession and U.S. auditing standards for audits of private companies; federal, state and local governments; and non-profit organizations.

Approximately 40% of its members are engaged in the practice of public accounting, in areas such as auditing, accounting, taxation, general business consulting, business valuation, personal financial planning and business technology.

   a. Other postemployment benefits
   b. American Institute of Certified Public Accountants
   c. ABC Television Network
   d. AIG

10. An _____ is a practitioner of accountancy, which is the measurement, disclosure or provision of assurance about financial information that helps managers, investors, tax authorities and other decision makers make resource allocation decisions.

The word '_____' is derived from the French 'Compter' which took its origin from the Latin 'Computare'. The word was formerly written in English as 'Accomptant', but in process of time the word, which was always pronounced by dropping the 'p', became gradually changed both in pronunciation and in orthography to its present form.

   a. AIG
   b. ABC Television Network
   c. AMEX
   d. Accountant

11. The general definition of an _____ is an evaluation of a person, organization, system, process, project or product. _____s are performed to ascertain the validity and reliability of information; also to provide an assessment of a system's internal control. The goal of an _____ is to express an opinion on the person/organization/system (etc) in question, under evaluation based on work done on a test basis.

a. Audit regime
b. Institute of Chartered Accountants of India
c. Audit
d. Assurance service

12. The _____ is a professional organization headquartered in Montvale, New Jersey consisting of over 70,000 members worldwide. The IMA is dedicated to advancing the role of the management accountant and financial manager within the business organization, and provides relevant professional certification.

The IMA awards the Certified Management Accountant (CMA) designation in the United States.

a. Emerging technologies
b. International Accounting Standards Committee
c. American Accounting Association
d. Institute of Management Accountants

13. _____ is concerned with the provisions and use of accounting information to managers within organizations, to provide them with the basis to make informed business decisions that will allow them to be better equipped in their management and control functions.

In contrast to financial accountancy information, _____ information is:

- usually confidential and used by management, instead of publicly reported;
- forward-looking, instead of historical;
- pragmatically computed using extensive management information systems and internal controls, instead of complying with accounting standards.

This is because of the different emphasis: _____ information is used within an organization, typically for decision-making.

a. Management accounting
b. Governmental accounting
c. Nonassurance services
d. Grenzplankostenrechnung

Chapter 1. Ethical Issues in Advanced Accounting

14. _____ Corporation of America was a Los Angeles-based U.S. financial conglomerate that marketed a package of mutual funds and life insurance to private individuals in the 1960s and 70s. It collapsed in scandal in 1973 after ex-employee Ronald Secrist and securities analyst Ray Dirks blew the whistle on massive accounting fraud, including a computer system dedicated exclusively to creating and maintaining fictitious insurance policies. Investigation found that from 1964 onward, as many as 100 company employees had engaged in organized deception of investors, auditors, reinsurers and regulatory authorities.
    a. ABC Television Network
    b. AIG
    c. Equity Funding
    d. AMEX

15. A _____ is a fungible, negotiable instrument representing financial value. they are broadly categorized into debt securities (such as banknotes, bonds and debentures), and equity securities; e.g., common stocks. The company or other entity issuing the _____ is called the issuer.
    a. Tracking stock
    b. BMC Software, Inc.
    c. 3M Company
    d. Security

16. The U.S. _____ is an independent agency of the United States government which holds primary responsibility for enforcing the federal securities laws and regulating the securities industry, the nation's stock and options exchanges, and other electronic securities markets. The SEC was created by section 4 of the Securities Exchange Act of 1934 (now codified as 15 U.S.C. §§ 78d and commonly referred to as the 1934 Act.)
    a. BMC Software, Inc.
    b. 3M Company
    c. BNSF Railway
    d. Securities and Exchange Commission

17. The _____ is currently the source of generally accepted accounting principles (GAAP) used by State and Local governments in the [[United States of America]]. As with most of the entities involved in creating GAAP in the United States, it is a private, non-governmental organization.

The _____ is subject to oversight by the Financial Accounting Foundation (FAF), which selects the members of the _____ and the Financial Accounting Standards Board, and funds both organizations.

a. Governmental Accounting Standards Board
b. National Conference of Commissioners on Uniform State Laws
c. Fannie Mae
d. Multinational corporation

18. _____ were published by Accounting Principles Board (APB.) The board was created by American Institute of Certified Public Accountants (AICPA) in 1959 and was replaced by Financial Accounting Standards Board (FASB) in 1973. Its mission was to develop an overall conceptual framework of US generally accepted accounting principles (US GAAP.)
   a. ABC Television Network
   b. AIG
   c. Accounting Principles Board Opinions
   d. AMEX

19. The _____ is the former authoritative body of the American Institute of Certified Public Accountants (AICPA.) It was created by the American Institute of Certified Public Accountants in 1959 and issued pronouncements on accounting principles until 1973, when it was replaced by the Financial Accounting Standards Board (FASB.)

The _____ was disbanded in the hopes that the smaller, fully-independent FASB could more effectively create accounting standards.

   a. International Federation of Accountants
   b. Institute of Management Accountants
   c. American Payroll Association
   d. Accounting Principles Board

Chapter 2. Partnerships: Organization and Operation

1. In the commercial and legal parlance of most countries, a _____ or simply a partnership, refers to an association of persons or an unincorporated company with the following major features:

   - Created by agreement, proof of existence and estoppel.
   - Formed by two or more persons
   - The owners are all personally liable for any legal actions and debts the company may face

   It is a partnership in which partners share equally in both responsibility and liability.

   Partnerships have certain default characteristics relating to both the relationship between the individual partners and (b) the relationship between the partnership and the outside world. The former can generally be overridden by agreement between the partners, whereas the latter generally cannot be.

   The assets of the business are owned on behalf of the other partners, and they are each personally liable, jointly and severally, for business debts, taxes or tortious liability.

   a. Dow Jones ' Company
   b. Governmental Accounting Standards Board
   c. Multinational corporation
   d. General partnership

2. A _____ is a type of business entity in which partners (owners) share with each other the profits or losses of the business undertaking in which all have invested. _____s are often favored over corporations for taxation purposes, as the _____ structure does not generally incur a tax on profits before it is distributed to the partners (i.e. there is no dividend tax levied.) However, depending on the _____ structure and the jurisdiction in which it operates, owners of a _____ may be exposed to greater personal liability than they would as shareholders of a corporation.
   a. National Information Infrastructure Protection Act
   b. Corporate governance
   c. Resource Conservation and Recovery Act
   d. Partnership

3. A _____ is a fungible, negotiable instrument representing financial value. they are broadly categorized into debt securities (such as banknotes, bonds and debentures), and equity securities; e.g., common stocks. The company or other entity issuing the _____ is called the issuer.
   a. BMC Software, Inc.
   b. 3M Company
   c. Tracking stock
   d. Security

Chapter 2. Partnerships: Organization and Operation

4. The U.S. _____ is an independent agency of the United States government which holds primary responsibility for enforcing the federal securities laws and regulating the securities industry, the nation's stock and options exchanges, and other electronic securities markets. The SEC was created by section 4 of the Securities Exchange Act of 1934 (now codified as 15 U.S.C. ÂÂ§ 78d and commonly referred to as the 1934 Act.)
    a. 3M Company
    b. Securities and Exchange Commission
    c. BNSF Railway
    d. BMC Software, Inc.

5. The _____ , which includes revisions that are sometimes called the Revised _____, is a uniform act (similar to a model statute), proposed by the National Conference of Commissioners on Uniform State Laws ('NCCUSL') for the governance of business partnerships by U.S. States. Several versions of _____ have been promulgated by the NCCUSL, the earliest having been put forth in 1914, and the most recent in 1997.

    The NCCUSL's first revision of _____ was promulgated in 1992 and amended in 1993 and 1994.

    a. ABC Television Network
    b. Uniform Partnership Act
    c. AMEX
    d. AIG

6. _____ is a concept whereby a person's financial liability is limited to a fixed sum, most commonly the value of a person's investment in a company or partnership with _____. A shareholder in a limited company is not personally liable for any of the debts of the company, other than for the value of his investment in that company. The same is true for the members of a _____ partnership and the limited partners in a limited partnership.
    a. Joint venture
    b. Due diligence
    c. Burden of proof
    d. Limited liability

7. A _____ is a partnership in which some or all partners (depending on the jurisdiction) have limited liability. It therefore exhibits elements of partnerships and corporations. In an _____ one partner is not responsible or liable for another partner's misconduct or negligence.
    a. Privately held
    b. Dow Jones ' Company
    c. Financial Accounting Standards Board
    d. Limited liability partnership

Chapter 2. Partnerships: Organization and Operation

8. In financial accounting, a _____ is defined as an obligation of an entity arising from past transactions or events, the settlement of which may result in the transfer or use of assets, provision of services or other yielding of economic benefits in the future.
   a. Corporate governance
   b. Vested
   c. False Claims Act
   d. Liability

9. _____ is equal to the income that a firm has after subtracting costs and expenses from the total revenue. _____ can be distributed among holders of common stock as a dividend or held by the firm as retained earnings.

The items deducted will typically include tax expense, financing expense (interest expense), and minority interest. Likewise, preferred stock dividends will be subtracted too, though they are not an expense.

   a. Generally accepted accounting principles
   b. Long-term liabilities
   c. Matching principle
   d. Net income

10. _____ is a doctrine in the tax law of the United States under which a transaction must have an economic purpose aside from reduction of tax liability in order to be considered valid. This doctrine is used to determine whether tax shelters, or strategies used to reduce tax liability, are considered 'abusive' by the Internal Revenue Service.
   a. Excise stamp
   b. Occupational privilege tax
   c. ABC Television Network
   d. Economic substance

11. _____ were published by Accounting Principles Board (APB.) The board was created by American Institute of Certified Public Accountants (AICPA) in 1959 and was replaced by Financial Accounting Standards Board (FASB) in 1973. Its mission was to develop an overall conceptual framework of US generally accepted accounting principles (US GAAP.)
   a. AIG
   b. AMEX
   c. ABC Television Network
   d. Accounting Principles Board Opinions

12. _____ are formal records of a business' financial activities.

In British English, including United Kingdom company law, _____ are often referred to as accounts, although the term _____ is also used, particularly by accountants.

_____ provide an overview of a business' financial condition in both short and long term.

a. Financial statements
b. Statement of retained earnings
c. Notes to the financial statements
d. 3M Company

13. A _____ is a type of debt Like all debt instruments, a _____ entails the redistribution of financial assets over time, between the lender and the borrower.
a. Debenture
b. Loan to value
c. Lender
d. Loan

14. The _____ is currently the source of generally accepted accounting principles (GAAP) used by State and Local governments in the [[United States of America]]. As with most of the entities involved in creating GAAP in the United States, it is a private, non-governmental organization.

The _____ is subject to oversight by the Financial Accounting Foundation (FAF), which selects the members of the _____ and the Financial Accounting Standards Board, and funds both organizations.

a. Governmental Accounting Standards Board
b. Fannie Mae
c. National Conference of Commissioners on Uniform State Laws
d. Multinational corporation

15. _____ are financial statements that factor the holding company's subsidiaries into its aggregated accounting figure. It is a representation of how the holding company is doing as a group. The consolidated accounts should provide a true and fair view of the financial and operating conditions of the group.
a. Consolidated financial statements
b. Committee on Accounting Procedure
c. Redemption value
d. Replacement cost

Chapter 2. Partnerships: Organization and Operation

16. _____ are journal entries made at the end of an accounting period to transfer temporary accounts to permanent accounts. An 'income summary' account may be used to show the balance between revenue and expenses, or they could be directly closed against retained earnings where dividend payments will be deducted from. This process is used to reset the balance of these temporary accounts to zero for the next accounting period.

   a. Treasury stock
   b. Trial balance
   c. FIFO and LIFO accounting
   d. Closing entries

17. In monetary economics _____ can refer either to a particular _____, for example British Pounds or United States Dollars, or, to the coins and banknotes of a particular _____, which actually form only a small part of the monetary base of a nation's money supply. The other part of a nation's money supply consists of money deposited in banks (sometimes called deposit money), ownership of which can be transferred by means of checks (cheques in the United Kingdom and Australia) or other forms of money transfer such as credit and debit cards. Deposit money and _____ are 'money' in the sense that both are acceptable as a means of exchange, but money need not necessarily be '_____'.

   a. BMC Software, Inc.
   b. 3M Company
   c. BNSF Railway
   d. Currency

18. _____ is the state or fact of exclusive rights and control over property, which may be an object, land/real estate or intellectual property. An _____ right is also referred to as title.

   _____ is the key building block in the development of the capitalist socio-economic system.

   a. ABC Television Network
   b. Encumbrance
   c. Administrative proceeding
   d. Ownership

19. A _____ is a form of partnership similar to a general partnership, except that in addition to one or more general partners (GPs), there are one or more limited partners (_____s.) It is a partnership in which only one partner is required to be a general partner.

The GPs are, in all major respects, in the same legal position as partners in a conventional firm, i.e. they have management control, share the right to use partnership property, share the profits of the firm in predefined proportions, and have joint and several liability for the debts of the partnership.

Chapter 2. Partnerships: Organization and Operation

a. Dow Jones ' Company
b. Minority interest
c. Debenture
d. Limited Partnership

20. _____, Quarterly Report Pursuant to Section 13 or 15(d) of the Securities Exchange Act of 1934, is an SEC filing that must be filed quarterly with the US Securities and Exchange Commission. It contains similar information to the annual form 10-K, however the information is generally less detailed, and the financial statements are generally unaudited. Information for the final quarter of a firm's fiscal year is included in the 10-K, so only three 10-Q filings are made each year.
a. 3M Company
b. Form 8-K
c. Form 20-F
d. Form 10-Q

21. A _____ is an annual report required by the U.S. Securities and Exchange Commission (SEC), that gives a comprehensive summary of a public company's performance. Although similarly named, the annual report on _____ is distinct from the often glossy 'annual report to shareholders', which a company must send to its shareholders when it holds an annual meeting to elect directors (though some companies combine the annual report and the 10-K into one document.) The 10-K includes information such as company history, organizational structure, executive compensation, equity, subsidiaries, and audited financial statements, among other information.
a. Form 8-K
b. 3M Company
c. Form 10-K
d. Form 10-Q

22. The _____ is a private, not-for-profit organization whose primary purpose is to develop generally accepted accounting principles (GAAP) within the United States in the public's interest. The Securities and Exchange Commission (SEC) designated the _____ as the organization responsible for setting accounting standards for public companies in the U.S. It was created in 1973, replacing the Accounting Principles Board and the Committee on Accounting Procedure of the American Institute of Certified Public Accountants. The _____'s mission is 'to establish and improve standards of financial accounting and reporting for the guidance and education of the public, including issuers, auditors, and users of financial information.'

The _____ is not a governmental body.

a. Public company
b. Fannie Mae
c. Governmental Accounting Standards Board
d. Financial Accounting Standards Board

Chapter 3. Partnership Liquidation and Incorporation; Joint Ventures

1. In law, _____ refers to the process by which a company (or part of a company) is brought to an end, and the assets and property of the company redistributed. _____ can also be referred to as winding-up or dissolution, although dissolution technically refers to the last stage of _____. The process of _____ also arises when customs, an authority or agency in a country responsible for collecting and safeguarding customs duties, determines the final computation or ascertainment of the duties or drawback accruing on an entry.

   a. BMC Software, Inc.
   b. 3M Company
   c. Bankruptcy protection
   d. Liquidation

2. A _____ is a type of business entity in which partners (owners) share with each other the profits or losses of the business undertaking in which all have invested. _____s are often favored over corporations for taxation purposes, as the _____ structure does not generally incur a tax on profits before it is distributed to the partners (i.e. there is no dividend tax levied.) However, depending on the _____ structure and the jurisdiction in which it operates, owners of a _____ may be exposed to greater personal liability than they would as shareholders of a corporation.

   a. Corporate governance
   b. National Information Infrastructure Protection Act
   c. Resource Conservation and Recovery Act
   d. Partnership

3. _____ is generally understood in financial circles as the point at which revenue is recognized, typically through a transaction which involves the exchange of an asset, product, or service for cash or its equivalents.

   This approach gives the accounting division a strictly objective basis for changing the books. For example, a homeowner may believe that his house has grown in value during a strong market, or fallen in value during a weak market, but until the house is actually sold for a specific price to a specific buyer, the change in value can only be estimated and is considered unrealized.

   a. Total-factor productivity
   b. Valuation
   c. Merck ' Co., Inc.
   d. Realization

4. _____ means the inability to pay one's debts as they fall due. Usually used in Business terms, _____ refers to the inability for a 'limited liability' company to pay off debts.

   This is defined in two different ways:

   Cash flow _____ -
   Unable to pay debts as they fall due.

Chapter 3. Partnership Liquidation and Incorporation; Joint Ventures

a. AIG
b. Interest
c. Insolvency
d. ABC Television Network

5. In business and accounting, _____ are everything of value that is owned by a person or company. It is a claim on the property your income of a borrower. The balance sheet of a firm records the monetary value of the _____ owned by the firm.

a. Accounts receivable
b. Earnings before interest, taxes, depreciation and amortization
c. Assets
d. Accrual basis accounting

6. A _____ is the transfer of wealth from one party (such as a person or company) to another. A _____ is usually made in exchange for the provision of goods, services or both, or to fulfill a legal obligation.

The simplest and oldest form of _____ is barter, the exchange of one good or service for another.

a. Payment
b. Payee
c. BMC Software, Inc.
d. 3M Company

7. _____ are financial statements that factor the holding company's subsidiaries into its aggregated accounting figure. It is a representation of how the holding company is doing as a group. The consolidated accounts should provide a true and fair view of the financial and operating conditions of the group.

a. Consolidated financial statements
b. Committee on Accounting Procedure
c. Redemption value
d. Replacement cost

8. _____ are journal entries made at the end of an accounting period to transfer temporary accounts to permanent accounts. An 'income summary' account may be used to show the balance between revenue and expenses, or they could be directly closed against retained earnings where dividend payments will be deducted from. This process is used to reset the balance of these temporary accounts to zero for the next accounting period.

Chapter 3. Partnership Liquidation and Incorporation; Joint Ventures

  a. Treasury stock
  b. Closing entries
  c. FIFO and LIFO accounting
  d. Trial balance

9. In monetary economics _____ can refer either to a particular _____, for example British Pounds or United States Dollars, or, to the coins and banknotes of a particular _____, which actually form only a small part of the monetary base of a nation's money supply. The other part of a nation's money supply consists of money deposited in banks (sometimes called deposit money), ownership of which can be transferred by means of checks (cheques in the United Kingdom and Australia) or other forms of money transfer such as credit and debit cards. Deposit money and _____ are 'money' in the sense that both are acceptable as a means of exchange, but money need not necessarily be '_____'.

  a. BNSF Railway
  b. BMC Software, Inc.
  c. 3M Company
  d. Currency

10. _____ are formal records of a business' financial activities.

In British English, including United Kingdom company law, _____ are often referred to as accounts, although the term _____ is also used, particularly by accountants.

_____ provide an overview of a business' financial condition in both short and long term.

  a. Notes to the financial statements
  b. Statement of retained earnings
  c. 3M Company
  d. Financial statements

11. The _____ is a private, not-for-profit organization whose primary purpose is to develop generally accepted accounting principles (GAAP) within the United States in the public's interest. The Securities and Exchange Commission (SEC) designated the _____ as the organization responsible for setting accounting standards for public companies in the U.S. It was created in 1973, replacing the Accounting Principles Board and the Committee on Accounting Procedure of the American Institute of Certified Public Accountants. The _____'s mission is 'to establish and improve standards of financial accounting and reporting for the guidance and education of the public, including issuers, auditors, and users of financial information.'

The _____ is not a governmental body.

a. Financial Accounting Standards Board
b. Governmental Accounting Standards Board
c. Fannie Mae
d. Public company

12. _____ is a concept whereby a person's financial liability is limited to a fixed sum, most commonly the value of a person's investment in a company or partnership with _____. A shareholder in a limited company is not personally liable for any of the debts of the company, other than for the value of his investment in that company. The same is true for the members of a _____ partnership and the limited partners in a limited partnership.
   a. Joint venture
   b. Limited liability
   c. Due diligence
   d. Burden of proof

13. A _____ is a partnership in which some or all partners (depending on the jurisdiction) have limited liability. It therefore exhibits elements of partnerships and corporations. In an _____ one partner is not responsible or liable for another partner's misconduct or negligence.
   a. Privately held
   b. Dow Jones ' Company
   c. Limited liability partnership
   d. Financial Accounting Standards Board

14. In financial accounting, a _____ is defined as an obligation of an entity arising from past transactions or events, the settlement of which may result in the transfer or use of assets, provision of services or other yielding of economic benefits in the future.
   a. False Claims Act
   b. Vested
   c. Corporate governance
   d. Liability

15. _____ were published by Accounting Principles Board (APB.) The board was created by American Institute of Certified Public Accountants (AICPA) in 1959 and was replaced by Financial Accounting Standards Board (FASB) in 1973. Its mission was to develop an overall conceptual framework of US generally accepted accounting principles (US GAAP.)

Chapter 3. Partnership Liquidation and Incorporation; Joint Ventures

a. AIG
b. AMEX
c. ABC Television Network
d. Accounting Principles Board Opinions

16. The _____ is the former authoritative body of the American Institute of Certified Public Accountants (AICPA.) It was created by the American Institute of Certified Public Accountants in 1959 and issued pronouncements on accounting principles until 1973, when it was replaced by the Financial Accounting Standards Board (FASB.)

The _____ was disbanded in the hopes that the smaller, fully-independent FASB could more effectively create accounting standards.

a. International Federation of Accountants
b. Accounting Principles Board
c. American Payroll Association
d. Institute of Management Accountants

17. A _____ is an entity formed between two or more parties to undertake economic activity together. The parties agree to create a new entity by both contributing equity, and they then share in the revenues, expenses, and control of the enterprise. The venture can be for one specific project only, or a continuing business relationship such as the Fuji Xerox _____.
a. Fraud Enforcement and Recovery Act
b. Chief Financial Officers Act of 1990
c. Pre-emption right
d. Joint venture

18. _____ methods are means of managing inventory and financial matters involving the money a company ties up within inventory of produced goods, raw materials, parts, components, or feed stocks. FIFO stands for first-in, first-out, meaning that the oldest inventory items are recorded as sold first. LIFO stands for last-in, first-out, meaning that the most recently purchased items are recorded as sold first.
a. Reorder point
b. Finished good
c. 3M Company
d. FIFO and LIFO accounting

Chapter 3. Partnership Liquidation and Incorporation; Joint Ventures

19. The general definition of an _____ is an evaluation of a person, organization, system, process, project or product. _____s are performed to ascertain the validity and reliability of information; also to provide an assessment of a system's internal control. The goal of an _____ is to express an opinion on the person/organization/system (etc) in question, under evaluation based on work done on a test basis.
    a. Assurance service
    b. Audit regime
    c. Institute of Chartered Accountants of India
    d. Audit

20. _____ in accounting is the process of treating equity investments, usually 20-50%, in associate companies. The investor keeps such equities as an asset. Proportional share of associate company's net income increases the investment, and proportional payment of dividends decreases it.
    a. Equity method
    b. AIG
    c. Out-of-pocket
    d. ABC Television Network

21. _____, Quarterly Report Pursuant to Section 13 or 15(d) of the Securities Exchange Act of 1934, is an SEC filing that must be filed quarterly with the US Securities and Exchange Commission. It contains similar information to the annual form 10-K, however the information is generally less detailed, and the financial statements are generally unaudited. Information for the final quarter of a firm's fiscal year is included in the 10-K, so only three 10-Q filings are made each year.
    a. 3M Company
    b. Form 20-F
    c. Form 8-K
    d. Form 10-Q

22. A _____ is a fungible, negotiable instrument representing financial value. they are broadly categorized into debt securities (such as banknotes, bonds and debentures), and equity securities; e.g., common stocks. The company or other entity issuing the _____ is called the issuer.
    a. 3M Company
    b. Security
    c. Tracking stock
    d. BMC Software, Inc.

23. The _____ of 1934 is a law governing the secondary trading of securities (stocks, bonds, and debentures) in the United States of America. The Act, 48 Stat. 881 (enacted June 6, 1934), codified at 15 U.S.C.

a. 3M Company
b. Securities Exchange Act
c. BNSF Railway
d. BMC Software, Inc.

24. The _____ is a law governing the secondary trading of securities (stocks, bonds, and debentures) in the United States of America. The Act, 48 Stat. 881 (enacted June 6, 1934), codified at 15 U.S.C.
a. Securities Exchange Act of 1934
b. BNSF Railway
c. 3M Company
d. BMC Software, Inc.

Chapter 4. Accounting for Branches; Combined Financial Statements

1. A _____, in business matters, is an entity that is controlled by a bigger and more powerful entity. The controlled entity is called a company, corporation, or limited liability company, and the controlling entity is called its parent (or the parent company.) The reason for this distinction is that a lone company cannot be a _____ of any organization; only an entity representing a legal fiction as a separate entity can be a _____.
    a. BMC Software, Inc.
    b. 3M Company
    c. Parent company
    d. Subsidiary

2. A _____ is a bond which is worth a certain monetary value and which may only be spent for specific reasons or on specific goods. Examples include -- but are not limited to -- housing, travel and food _____s. The term _____ is also a synonym for receipt, and is often used to refer to receipts used as evidence of, for example, the declaration that a service has been performed or that an expenditure has been made.
    a. BMC Software, Inc.
    b. Source document
    c. Voucher
    d. 3M Company

3. The U.S. _____ is an independent agency of the United States government which holds primary responsibility for enforcing the federal securities laws and regulating the securities industry, the nation's stock and options exchanges, and other electronic securities markets. The SEC was created by section 4 of the Securities Exchange Act of 1934 (now codified as 15 U.S.C. ÂÂ§ 78d and commonly referred to as the 1934 Act.)
    a. BMC Software, Inc.
    b. BNSF Railway
    c. 3M Company
    d. Securities and Exchange Commission

4. In economics, business, retail, and accounting, a _____ is the value of money that has been used up to produce something, and hence is not available for use anymore. In economics, a _____ is an alternative that is given up as a result of a decision. In business, the _____ may be one of acquisition, in which case the amount of money expended to acquire it is counted as _____.
    a. Cost of quality
    b. Cost allocation
    c. Prime cost
    d. Cost

5. _____ are financial statements that factor the holding company's subsidiaries into its aggregated accounting figure. It is a representation of how the holding company is doing as a group. The consolidated accounts should provide a true and fair view of the financial and operating conditions of the group.

Chapter 4. Accounting for Branches; Combined Financial Statements

a. Redemption value
b. Committee on Accounting Procedure
c. Consolidated financial statements
d. Replacement cost

6. _____ is a company's financial statement that indicates how the revenue is transformed into the net income The purpose of the _____ is to show managers and investors whether the company made or lost money during the period being reported.

The important thing to remember about an _____ is that it represents a period of time.

a. AMEX
b. ABC Television Network
c. AIG
d. Income statement

7. _____ are journal entries made at the end of an accounting period to transfer temporary accounts to permanent accounts. An 'income summary' account may be used to show the balance between revenue and expenses, or they could be directly closed against retained earnings where dividend payments will be deducted from. This process is used to reset the balance of these temporary accounts to zero for the next accounting period.

a. FIFO and LIFO accounting
b. Closing entries
c. Treasury stock
d. Trial balance

8. In monetary economics _____ can refer either to a particular _____, for example British Pounds or United States Dollars, or, to the coins and banknotes of a particular _____, which actually form only a small part of the monetary base of a nation's money supply. The other part of a nation's money supply consists of money deposited in banks (sometimes called deposit money), ownership of which can be transferred by means of checks (cheques in the United Kingdom and Australia) or other forms of money transfer such as credit and debit cards. Deposit money and _____ are 'money' in the sense that both are acceptable as a means of exchange, but money need not necessarily be '_____'.

a. 3M Company
b. BNSF Railway
c. BMC Software, Inc.
d. Currency

Chapter 4. Accounting for Branches; Combined Financial Statements

9. In accounting, _____ has a very specific meaning. It is an outflow of cash or other valuable assets from a person or company to another person or company. This outflow of cash is generally one side of a trade for products or services that have equal or better current or future value to the buyer than to the seller.

   a. AMEX
   b. ABC Television Network
   c. AIG
   d. Expense

10. _____ are formal records of a business' financial activities.

    In British English, including United Kingdom company law, _____ are often referred to as accounts, although the term _____ is also used, particularly by accountants.

    _____ provide an overview of a business' financial condition in both short and long term.

    a. Financial statements
    b. Notes to the financial statements
    c. Statement of retained earnings
    d. 3M Company

11. The _____ is a private, not-for-profit organization whose primary purpose is to develop generally accepted accounting principles (GAAP) within the United States in the public's interest. The Securities and Exchange Commission (SEC) designated the _____ as the organization responsible for setting accounting standards for public companies in the U.S. It was created in 1973, replacing the Accounting Principles Board and the Committee on Accounting Procedure of the American Institute of Certified Public Accountants. The _____'s mission is 'to establish and improve standards of financial accounting and reporting for the guidance and education of the public, including issuers, auditors, and users of financial information.'

    The _____ is not a governmental body.

    a. Fannie Mae
    b. Public company
    c. Governmental Accounting Standards Board
    d. Financial Accounting Standards Board

Chapter 5. Business Combinations

1. _____ are financial statements that factor the holding company's subsidiaries into its aggregated accounting figure. It is a representation of how the holding company is doing as a group. The consolidated accounts should provide a true and fair view of the financial and operating conditions of the group.

    a. Committee on Accounting Procedure
    b. Redemption value
    c. Consolidated financial statements
    d. Replacement cost

2. _____ in a corporation means to have control of a large enough block of voting stock shares in a company such that no one stock holder or coalition of stock holders can successfully oppose a motion. In theory this normally means that _____ would be 50% of the voting shares plus one.

    In practice, though, _____ can be far less than that, as it is rare that 100% of a company's voting shareholders actively vote.

    a. Preferred stock
    b. Public offering
    c. Participating preferred stock
    d. Controlling interest

3. _____ are formal records of a business' financial activities.

    In British English, including United Kingdom company law, _____ are often referred to as accounts, although the term _____ is also used, particularly by accountants.

    _____ provide an overview of a business' financial condition in both short and long term.

    a. Statement of retained earnings
    b. Notes to the financial statements
    c. Financial statements
    d. 3M Company

4. _____ is a fee paid on borrowed assets. It is the price paid for the use of borrowed money, or, money earned by deposited funds. Assets that are sometimes lent with _____ include money, shares, consumer goods through hire purchase, major assets such as aircraft, and even entire factories in finance lease arrangements. The _____ is calculated upon the value of the assets in the same manner as upon money.

Chapter 5. Business Combinations

a. Insolvency
b. ABC Television Network
c. AIG
d. Interest

5. An _____ is the buying of one company by another. An _____ may be friendly or hostile. In the former case, the companies cooperate in negotiations; in the latter case, the takeover target is unwilling to be bought or the target's board has no prior knowledge of the offer. _____ usually refers to a purchase of a smaller firm by a larger one. Sometimes, however, a smaller firm will acquire management control of a larger or longer established company and keep its name for the combined entity. This is known as a reverse takeover.
   a. AIG
   b. Acquisition
   c. AMEX
   d. ABC Television Network

6. The U.S. _____ is an independent agency of the United States government which holds primary responsibility for enforcing the federal securities laws and regulating the securities industry, the nation's stock and options exchanges, and other electronic securities markets. The SEC was created by section 4 of the Securities Exchange Act of 1934 (now codified as 15 U.S.C. ÂÂ§ 78d and commonly referred to as the 1934 Act.)
   a. BMC Software, Inc.
   b. Securities and Exchange Commission
   c. BNSF Railway
   d. 3M Company

7. In business or economics a _____ is a combination of two companies into one larger company. Such actions are commonly voluntary and involve stock swap or cash payment to the target. Stock swap is often used as it allows the shareholders of the two companies to share the risk involved in the deal. A _____ can resemble a takeover but result in a new company name (often combining the names of the original companies) and in new branding; in some cases, terming the combination a '_____' rather than an acquisition is done purely for political or marketing reasons.
   a. BMC Software, Inc.
   b. BNSF Railway
   c. 3M Company
   d. Merger

8. The _____ is a private, not-for-profit organization whose primary purpose is to develop generally accepted accounting principles (GAAP) within the United States in the public's interest. The Securities and Exchange Commission (SEC) designated the _____ as the organization responsible for setting accounting standards for public companies in the U.S. It was created in 1973, replacing the Accounting Principles Board and the Committee on Accounting Procedure of the American Institute of Certified Public Accountants. The _____'s mission is 'to establish and improve standards of financial accounting and reporting for the guidance and education of the public, including issuers, auditors, and users of financial information.'

The _____ is not a governmental body.

   a. Financial Accounting Standards Board
   b. Public company
   c. Governmental Accounting Standards Board
   d. Fannie Mae

9. The _____ is the national, professional association of CPAs in the United States, with more than 330,000 members, including CPAs in business and industry, public practice, government, and education; student affiliates; and international associates. It sets ethical standards for the profession and U.S. auditing standards for audits of private companies; federal, state and local governments; and non-profit organizations.

Approximately 40% of its members are engaged in the practice of public accounting, in areas such as auditing, accounting, taxation, general business consulting, business valuation, personal financial planning and business technology.

   a. Other postemployment benefits
   b. AIG
   c. American Institute of Certified Public Accountants
   d. ABC Television Network

10. _____ refers to a business or organization attempting to acquire goods or services to accomplish the goals of the enterprise. Though there are several organizations that attempt to set standards in the _____ process, processes can vary greatly between organizations. Typically the word e;_____e; is not used interchangeably with the word e;procuremente;, since procurement typically includes Expediting, Supplier Quality, and Traffic and Logistics (T'L) in addition to _____.

   a. Consignor
   b. Supply chain
   c. Free port
   d. Purchasing

11. _____ are journal entries made at the end of an accounting period to transfer temporary accounts to permanent accounts. An 'income summary' account may be used to show the balance between revenue and expenses, or they could be directly closed against retained earnings where dividend payments will be deducted from. This process is used to reset the balance of these temporary accounts to zero for the next accounting period.
   a. Closing entries
   b. Treasury stock
   c. FIFO and LIFO accounting
   d. Trial balance

12. In monetary economics _____ can refer either to a particular _____, for example British Pounds or United States Dollars, or, to the coins and banknotes of a particular _____, which actually form only a small part of the monetary base of a nation's money supply. The other part of a nation's money supply consists of money deposited in banks (sometimes called deposit money), ownership of which can be transferred by means of checks (cheques in the United Kingdom and Australia) or other forms of money transfer such as credit and debit cards. Deposit money and _____ are 'money' in the sense that both are acceptable as a means of exchange, but money need not necessarily be '_____'.
   a. 3M Company
   b. BMC Software, Inc.
   c. BNSF Railway
   d. Currency

Chapter 6. Consolidated Financial Statements: On Date of Business Combination

1. A _____, in business matters, is an entity that is controlled by a bigger and more powerful entity. The controlled entity is called a company, corporation, or limited liability company, and the controlling entity is called its parent (or the parent company.) The reason for this distinction is that a lone company cannot be a _____ of any organization; only an entity representing a legal fiction as a separate entity can be a _____.

   a. BMC Software, Inc.
   b. 3M Company
   c. Parent company
   d. Subsidiary

2. _____ are financial statements that factor the holding company's subsidiaries into its aggregated accounting figure. It is a representation of how the holding company is doing as a group. The consolidated accounts should provide a true and fair view of the financial and operating conditions of the group.

   a. Consolidated financial statements
   b. Replacement cost
   c. Redemption value
   d. Committee on Accounting Procedure

3. The _____ is a private, not-for-profit organization whose primary purpose is to develop generally accepted accounting principles (GAAP) within the United States in the public's interest. The Securities and Exchange Commission (SEC) designated the _____ as the organization responsible for setting accounting standards for public companies in the U.S. It was created in 1973, replacing the Accounting Principles Board and the Committee on Accounting Procedure of the American Institute of Certified Public Accountants. The _____'s mission is 'to establish and improve standards of financial accounting and reporting for the guidance and education of the public, including issuers, auditors, and users of financial information.'

   The _____ is not a governmental body.

   a. Financial Accounting Standards Board
   b. Governmental Accounting Standards Board
   c. Public company
   d. Fannie Mae

4. _____ in business is an accounting concept that refers to ownership of a company (subsidiary) that is less than 50% of outstanding shares. _____ belongs to other investors and is reported on the consolidated balance sheet of the owning company to reflect the claim on assets belonging to other, non-controlling shareholders. Also, _____ is reported on the consolidated income statement as a share of profit belonging to minority shareholders.

Chapter 6. Consolidated Financial Statements: On Date of Business Combination

a. Bankruptcy prediction
b. Credit memo
c. Minority interest
d. Subledger

5. _____ in a corporation means to have control of a large enough block of voting stock shares in a company such that no one stock holder or coalition of stock holders can successfully oppose a motion. In theory this normally means that _____ would be 50% of the voting shares plus one.

In practice, though, _____ can be far less than that, as it is rare that 100% of a company's voting shareholders actively vote.

a. Preferred stock
b. Public offering
c. Participating preferred stock
d. Controlling interest

6. _____ are formal records of a business' financial activities.

In British English, including United Kingdom company law, _____ are often referred to as accounts, although the term _____ is also used, particularly by accountants.

_____ provide an overview of a business' financial condition in both short and long term.

a. 3M Company
b. Notes to the financial statements
c. Statement of retained earnings
d. Financial statements

7. _____ is a fee paid on borrowed assets. It is the price paid for the use of borrowed money, or, money earned by deposited funds. Assets that are sometimes lent with _____ include money, shares, consumer goods through hire purchase, major assets such as aircraft, and even entire factories in finance lease arrangements. The _____ is calculated upon the value of the assets in the same manner as upon money.

a. Insolvency
b. AIG
c. Interest
d. ABC Television Network

Chapter 6. Consolidated Financial Statements: On Date of Business Combination

8. _____ is a doctrine in the tax law of the United States under which a transaction must have an economic purpose aside from reduction of tax liability in order to be considered valid. This doctrine is used to determine whether tax shelters, or strategies used to reduce tax liability, are considered 'abusive' by the Internal Revenue Service.
   a. Excise stamp
   b. ABC Television Network
   c. Occupational privilege tax
   d. Economic substance

9. A _____ is a fungible, negotiable instrument representing financial value. they are broadly categorized into debt securities (such as banknotes, bonds and debentures), and equity securities; e.g., common stocks. The company or other entity issuing the _____ is called the issuer.
   a. Tracking stock
   b. 3M Company
   c. BMC Software, Inc.
   d. Security

10. The U.S. _____ is an independent agency of the United States government which holds primary responsibility for enforcing the federal securities laws and regulating the securities industry, the nation's stock and options exchanges, and other electronic securities markets. The SEC was created by section 4 of the Securities Exchange Act of 1934 (now codified as 15 U.S.C. §§ 78d and commonly referred to as the 1934 Act.)
    a. BNSF Railway
    b. BMC Software, Inc.
    c. 3M Company
    d. Securities and Exchange Commission

11. _____ are journal entries made at the end of an accounting period to transfer temporary accounts to permanent accounts. An 'income summary' account may be used to show the balance between revenue and expenses, or they could be directly closed against retained earnings where dividend payments will be deducted from. This process is used to reset the balance of these temporary accounts to zero for the next accounting period.
    a. Trial balance
    b. Closing entries
    c. Treasury stock
    d. FIFO and LIFO accounting

Chapter 6. Consolidated Financial Statements: On Date of Business Combination

12. In monetary economics _____ can refer either to a particular _____, for example British Pounds or United States Dollars, or, to the coins and banknotes of a particular _____, which actually form only a small part of the monetary base of a nation's money supply. The other part of a nation's money supply consists of money deposited in banks (sometimes called deposit money), ownership of which can be transferred by means of checks (cheques in the United Kingdom and Australia) or other forms of money transfer such as credit and debit cards. Deposit money and _____ are 'money' in the sense that both are acceptable as a means of exchange, but money need not necessarily be '_____'.
    a. 3M Company
    b. BNSF Railway
    c. Currency
    d. BMC Software, Inc.

13. In financial accounting, a _____ or statement of financial position is a summary of a person's or organization's balances. Assets, liabilities and ownership equity are listed as of a specific date, such as the end of its financial year. A _____ is often described as a snapshot of a company's financial condition.
    a. Financial statements
    b. 3M Company
    c. Balance sheet
    d. Statement of retained earnings

Chapter 6. Consolidated Financial Statements: On Date of Business Combination

14. _____ means the giving out of information, either voluntarily or to be in compliance with legal regulations or workplace rules.

- In Computer security, full _____ means disclosing full information about vulnerabilities.
- In computing, _____ widget
- Journalism, full _____ refers to disclosing the interests of the writer which may bear on the subject being written about, for example, if the writer has worked with an interview subject in the past.

- In law:
    - The law of England and Wales, _____ refers to a process that may form part of legal proceedings, whereby parties inform to other parties the existence of any relevant documents that are, or have been, in their control. This compares with the process known as discovery in the course of legal proceedings in the United States.
    - In U.S. civil procedure (litigation rules for civil cases), _____ is a stage prior to trial. In civil cases, each party must disclose to the opposing party the following: names of witnesses which it may use to support its side, copies of documents (or mere description of these documents) in its control which it may use to support its side, computation of damages claimed, and certain insurance information. _____ is related to, but technically prior to, the discovery stage.
    - In Company law (known as 'corporate law' in the United States), _____ refers to giving out information about public or limited companies or their officers, which might be kept secret if the company was a private company or a partnership.

- In real property transactions, _____ refers to providing to a buyer information known to the seller or broker/agent concerning the condition or other aspects of real property that would affect the property's value or desirability. These rules regarding what information must be disclosed, and whether the information must be disclosed even if a buyer does not ask, vary from one jurisdiction to the next.

a. Tax harmonisation
b. Trailing
c. Controlled Foreign Corporations
d. Disclosure

Chapter 7. Consolidated Financial Statements: Subsequent to Date of Business Combination

1. _____ are financial statements that factor the holding company's subsidiaries into its aggregated accounting figure. It is a representation of how the holding company is doing as a group. The consolidated accounts should provide a true and fair view of the financial and operating conditions of the group.
   a. Redemption value
   b. Consolidated financial statements
   c. Committee on Accounting Procedure
   d. Replacement cost

2. _____ are journal entries made at the end of an accounting period to transfer temporary accounts to permanent accounts. An 'income summary' account may be used to show the balance between revenue and expenses, or they could be directly closed against retained earnings where dividend payments will be deducted from. This process is used to reset the balance of these temporary accounts to zero for the next accounting period.
   a. Treasury stock
   b. FIFO and LIFO accounting
   c. Trial balance
   d. Closing entries

3. _____ are formal records of a business' financial activities.

   In British English, including United Kingdom company law, _____ are often referred to as accounts, although the term _____ is also used, particularly by accountants.

   _____ provide an overview of a business' financial condition in both short and long term.

   a. 3M Company
   b. Notes to the financial statements
   c. Statement of retained earnings
   d. Financial statements

4. In economics, business, retail, and accounting, a _____ is the value of money that has been used up to produce something, and hence is not available for use anymore. In economics, a _____ is an alternative that is given up as a result of a decision. In business, the _____ may be one of acquisition, in which case the amount of money expended to acquire it is counted as _____.
   a. Cost allocation
   b. Cost
   c. Cost of quality
   d. Prime cost

5. _____ in accounting is the process of treating equity investments, usually 20-50%, in associate companies. The investor keeps such equities as an asset. Proportional share of associate company's net income increases the investment, and proportional payment of dividends decreases it.
   a. Out-of-pocket
   b. ABC Television Network
   c. AIG
   d. Equity method

Chapter 8. Consolidated Financial Statements: Intercompany Transactions

1. _____ are financial statements that factor the holding company's subsidiaries into its aggregated accounting figure. It is a representation of how the holding company is doing as a group. The consolidated accounts should provide a true and fair view of the financial and operating conditions of the group.

    a. Redemption value
    b. Committee on Accounting Procedure
    c. Replacement cost
    d. Consolidated financial statements

2. An _____ is the buying of one company by another. An _____ may be friendly or hostile. In the former case, the companies cooperate in negotiations; in the latter case, the takeover target is unwilling to be bought or the target's board has no prior knowledge of the offer. _____ usually refers to a purchase of a smaller firm by a larger one. Sometimes, however, a smaller firm will acquire management control of a larger or longer established company and keep its name for the combined entity. This is known as a reverse takeover.

    a. AIG
    b. ABC Television Network
    c. Acquisition
    d. AMEX

3. In finance, a _____ is a debt security, in which the authorized issuer owes the holders a debt and, depending on the terms of the _____, is obliged to pay interest (the coupon) and/or to repay the principal at a later date, termed maturity. It is a formal contract to repay borrowed money with interest at fixed intervals.

    Thus a _____ is like a loan: the issuer is the borrower, the _____ holder is the lender, and the coupon is the interest.

    a. Bond
    b. Coupon rate
    c. Zero-coupon bond
    d. Revenue bonds

4. _____ are formal records of a business' financial activities.

    In British English, including United Kingdom company law, _____ are often referred to as accounts, although the term _____ is also used, particularly by accountants.

    _____ provide an overview of a business' financial condition in both short and long term.

a. 3M Company
b. Notes to the financial statements
c. Statement of retained earnings
d. Financial statements

5. An _____ is a tax levied on the financial income of people, corporations, or other legal entities. Various _____ systems exist, with varying degrees of tax incidence. Income taxation can be progressive, proportional, or regressive.
   a. Individual Retirement Arrangement
   b. Income tax
   c. Implied level of government service
   d. Ordinary income

6. A _____ is the pinnacle activity involved in selling products or services in return for money or other compensation. It is an act of completion of a commercial activity.

A _____ is completed by the seller, the owner of the goods.

   a. Tertiary sector of economy
   b. Sale
   c. High yield stock
   d. Maturity

7. The U.S. _____ is an independent agency of the United States government which holds primary responsibility for enforcing the federal securities laws and regulating the securities industry, the nation's stock and options exchanges, and other electronic securities markets. The SEC was created by section 4 of the Securities Exchange Act of 1934 (now codified as 15 U.S.C. §§ 78d and commonly referred to as the 1934 Act.)
   a. BNSF Railway
   b. BMC Software, Inc.
   c. 3M Company
   d. Securities and Exchange Commission

8. In business and accounting, _____ are everything of value that is owned by a person or company. It is a claim on the property your income of a borrower. The balance sheet of a firm records the monetary value of the _____ owned by the firm.

Chapter 8. Consolidated Financial Statements: Intercompany Transactions

a. Accrual basis accounting
b. Assets
c. Accounts receivable
d. Earnings before interest, taxes, depreciation and amortization

9. A _____ is a contract conferring a right on one person to possess property belonging to another person (called a landlord or lessor) to the exclusion of the owner landlord. It is a rental agreement between landlord and tenant. The relationship between the tenant and the landlord is called a tenancy, and the right to possession by the tenant is sometimes called a leasehold interest.
    a. Model Code of Professional Responsibility
    b. Robinson-Patman Act
    c. Federal Sentencing Guidelines
    d. Lease

10. _____ are defined as identifiable non-monetary assets that cannot be seen, touched or physically measured, which are created through time and/or effort and that are identifiable as a separate asset. There are two primary forms of intangibles - legal intangibles (such as trade secrets (e.g., customer lists), copyrights, patents, trademarks, and goodwill) and competitive intangibles (such as knowledge activities (know-how, knowledge), collaboration activities, leverage activities, and structural activities.) Legal intangibles are known under the generic term intellectual property and generate legal property rights defensible in a court of law.
    a. Intangible assets
    b. Overhead
    c. AIG
    d. ABC Television Network

11. _____ is a fee paid on borrowed assets. It is the price paid for the use of borrowed money, or, money earned by deposited funds. Assets that are sometimes lent with _____ include money, shares, consumer goods through hire purchase, major assets such as aircraft, and even entire factories in finance lease arrangements. The _____ is calculated upon the value of the assets in the same manner as upon money.
    a. ABC Television Network
    b. Insolvency
    c. AIG
    d. Interest

12. _____ in business is an accounting concept that refers to ownership of a company (subsidiary) that is less than 50% of outstanding shares. _____ belongs to other investors and is reported on the consolidated balance sheet of the owning company to reflect the claim on assets belonging to other, non-controlling shareholders. Also, _____ is reported on the consolidated income statement as a share of profit belonging to minority shareholders.

a. Subledger
b. Bankruptcy prediction
c. Credit memo
d. Minority interest

Chapter 9. Consolidated Financial Statements: Income Taxes, Cash Flows, Acquisitions

1. _____ are financial statements that factor the holding company's subsidiaries into its aggregated accounting figure. It is a representation of how the holding company is doing as a group. The consolidated accounts should provide a true and fair view of the financial and operating conditions of the group.

    a. Redemption value
    b. Replacement cost
    c. Committee on Accounting Procedure
    d. Consolidated financial statements

2. The _____ is a private, not-for-profit organization whose primary purpose is to develop generally accepted accounting principles (GAAP) within the United States in the public's interest. The Securities and Exchange Commission (SEC) designated the _____ as the organization responsible for setting accounting standards for public companies in the U.S. It was created in 1973, replacing the Accounting Principles Board and the Committee on Accounting Procedure of the American Institute of Certified Public Accountants. The _____'s mission is 'to establish and improve standards of financial accounting and reporting for the guidance and education of the public, including issuers, auditors, and users of financial information.'

    The _____ is not a governmental body.

    a. Public company
    b. Governmental Accounting Standards Board
    c. Fannie Mae
    d. Financial Accounting Standards Board

3. _____ are formal records of a business' financial activities.

    In British English, including United Kingdom company law, _____ are often referred to as accounts, although the term _____ is also used, particularly by accountants.

    _____ provide an overview of a business' financial condition in both short and long term.

    a. Statement of retained earnings
    b. Notes to the financial statements
    c. Financial statements
    d. 3M Company

4. An _____ is a tax levied on the financial income of people, corporations, or other legal entities. Various _____ systems exist, with varying degrees of tax incidence. Income taxation can be progressive, proportional, or regressive.

Chapter 9. Consolidated Financial Statements: Income Taxes, Cash Flows, Acquisitions

a. Individual Retirement Arrangement
b. Ordinary income
c. Implied level of government service
d. Income tax

5. In business and accounting, _____ are everything of value that is owned by a person or company. It is a claim on the property your income of a borrower. The balance sheet of a firm records the monetary value of the _____ owned by the firm.

a. Earnings before interest, taxes, depreciation and amortization
b. Accrual basis accounting
c. Accounts receivable
d. Assets

6. _____, also called fair price (in a commonplace conflation of the two distinct concepts), is a concept used in finance and economics, defined as a rational and unbiased estimate of the potential market price of a good, service, or asset, taking into account such objective factors as:

- acquisition/production/distribution costs, replacement costs, or costs of close substitutes
- actual utility at a given level of development of social productive capability
- supply vs. demand

and subjective factors such as

- risk characteristics
- cost of capital
- individually perceived utility

In accounting, _____ is used as an estimate of the market value of an asset (or liability) for which a market price cannot be determined (usually because there is no established market for the asset.) Under GAAP (FAS 157), _____ is the amount at which the asset could be bought or sold in a current transaction between willing parties, or transferred to an equivalent party, other than in a liquidation sale. This is used for assets whose carrying value is based on mark-to-market valuations; for assets carried at historical cost, the _____ of the asset is not used. One example of where _____ is an issue is a College kitchen with a cost of $2 million which was built 5 years ago.

a. 3M Company
b. BMC Software, Inc.
c. BNSF Railway
d. Fair value

Chapter 9. Consolidated Financial Statements: Income Taxes, Cash Flows, Acquisitions

7. _____ is a fee paid on borrowed assets. It is the price paid for the use of borrowed money , or, money earned by deposited funds .Assets that are sometimes lent with _____ include money, shares, consumer goods through hire purchase, major assets such as aircraft, and even entire factories in finance lease arrangements. The _____ is calculated upon the value of the assets in the same manner as upon money.
   a. ABC Television Network
   b. Insolvency
   c. AIG
   d. Interest

8. _____ is the state or fact of exclusive rights and control over property, which may be an object, land/real estate or intellectual property. An _____ right is also referred to as title.

   _____ is the key building block in the development of the capitalist socio-economic system.

   a. Ownership
   b. ABC Television Network
   c. Administrative proceeding
   d. Encumbrance

9. A _____, in business matters, is an entity that is controlled by a bigger and more powerful entity. The controlled entity is called a company, corporation, or limited liability company, and the controlling entity is called its parent (or the parent company.) The reason for this distinction is that a lone company cannot be a _____ of any organization; only an entity representing a legal fiction as a separate entity can be a _____.
   a. BMC Software, Inc.
   b. Subsidiary
   c. 3M Company
   d. Parent company

10. _____ is a specific term used in companies' financial reporting from the company-whole point of view. Because that use excludes the effects of changing ownership interest, an economic measure of _____ is necessary for financial analysis from the shareholders' point of view

    _____ is defined by the Financial Accounting Standards Board, or FASB, as 'the change in equity [net assets] of a business enterprise during a period from transactions and other events and circumstances from nonowner sources. It includes all changes in equity during a period except those resulting from investments by owners and distributions to owners.'

    _____ is the sum of net income and other items that must bypass the income statement because they have not been realized, including items like an unrealized holding gain or loss from available for sale securities and foreign currency translation gains or losses.

42   Chapter 9. Consolidated Financial Statements: Income Taxes, Cash Flows, Acquisitions

a. BMC Software, Inc.
b. BNSF Railway
c. Comprehensive income
d. 3M Company

11. _____ is the balance of the amounts of cash being received and paid by a business during a defined period of time, sometimes tied to a specific project. Measurement of _____ can be used

- to evaluate the state or performance of a business or project.
- to determine problems with liquidity. Being profitable does not necessarily mean being liquid. A company can fail because of a shortage of cash, even while profitable.
- to project rate of returns. The time of _____s into and out of projects are used as inputs to financial models such as internal rate of return, and net present value.
- to examine income or growth of a business when it is believed that accrual accounting concepts do not represent economic realities. Alternately, _____ can be used to 'validate' the net income generated by accrual accounting.

_____ as a generic term may be used differently depending on context, and certain _____ definitions may be adapted by analysts and users for their own uses. Common terms include operating _____ and free _____.

a. Cash flow
b. Commercial paper
c. Controlling interest
d. Flow-through entity

12. In financial accounting, a _____ or Statement of cash flows is a financial statement that shows a company's flow of cash. The money coming into the business is called cash inflow, and money going out from the business is called cash outflow. The statement shows how changes in balance sheet and income accounts affect cash and cash equivalents, and breaks the analysis down to operating, investing, and financing activities.

a. 3M Company
b. BNSF Railway
c. BMC Software, Inc.
d. Cash flow statement

13. _____ were published by Accounting Principles Board (APB.) The board was created by American Institute of Certified Public Accountants (AICPA) in 1959 and was replaced by Financial Accounting Standards Board (FASB) in 1973. Its mission was to develop an overall conceptual framework of US generally accepted accounting principles (US GAAP.)

a. AMEX
b. Accounting Principles Board Opinions
c. ABC Television Network
d. AIG

14. The _____ is the former authoritative body of the American Institute of Certified Public Accountants (AICPA.) It was created by the American Institute of Certified Public Accountants in 1959 and issued pronouncements on accounting principles until 1973, when it was replaced by the Financial Accounting Standards Board (FASB.)

The _____ was disbanded in the hopes that the smaller, fully-independent FASB could more effectively create accounting standards.

a. Institute of Management Accountants
b. International Federation of Accountants
c. American Payroll Association
d. Accounting Principles Board

15. An _____ is the buying of one company by another. An _____ may be friendly or hostile. In the former case, the companies cooperate in negotiations; in the latter case, the takeover target is unwilling to be bought or the target's board has no prior knowledge of the offer. _____ usually refers to a purchase of a smaller firm by a larger one. Sometimes, however, a smaller firm will acquire management control of a larger or longer established company and keep its name for the combined entity. This is known as a reverse takeover.

a. AIG
b. ABC Television Network
c. AMEX
d. Acquisition

Chapter 10. Consolidated Financial Statements: Special Problems

1. _____ are financial statements that factor the holding company's subsidiaries into its aggregated accounting figure. It is a representation of how the holding company is doing as a group. The consolidated accounts should provide a true and fair view of the financial and operating conditions of the group.

   a. Redemption value
   b. Replacement cost
   c. Committee on Accounting Procedure
   d. Consolidated financial statements

2. The _____ is a private, not-for-profit organization whose primary purpose is to develop generally accepted accounting principles (GAAP) within the United States in the public's interest. The Securities and Exchange Commission (SEC) designated the _____ as the organization responsible for setting accounting standards for public companies in the U.S. It was created in 1973, replacing the Accounting Principles Board and the Committee on Accounting Procedure of the American Institute of Certified Public Accountants. The _____'s mission is 'to establish and improve standards of financial accounting and reporting for the guidance and education of the public, including issuers, auditors, and users of financial information.'

   The _____ is not a governmental body.

   a. Governmental Accounting Standards Board
   b. Public company
   c. Fannie Mae
   d. Financial Accounting Standards Board

3. _____ are formal records of a business' financial activities.

   In British English, including United Kingdom company law, _____ are often referred to as accounts, although the term _____ is also used, particularly by accountants.

   _____ provide an overview of a business' financial condition in both short and long term.

   a. Notes to the financial statements
   b. Statement of retained earnings
   c. 3M Company
   d. Financial statements

4. An _____ is the buying of one company by another. An _____ may be friendly or hostile. In the former case, the companies cooperate in negotiations; in the latter case, the takeover target is unwilling to be bought or the target's board has no prior knowledge of the offer. _____ usually refers to a purchase of a smaller firm by a larger one. Sometimes, however, a smaller firm will acquire management control of a larger or longer established company and keep its name for the combined entity. This is known as a reverse takeover.

Chapter 10. Consolidated Financial Statements: Special Problems 45

a. AIG
b. AMEX
c. Acquisition
d. ABC Television Network

5. _____ is a fee paid on borrowed assets. It is the price paid for the use of borrowed money, or, money earned by deposited funds. Assets that are sometimes lent with _____ include money, shares, consumer goods through hire purchase, major assets such as aircraft, and even entire factories in finance lease arrangements. The _____ is calculated upon the value of the assets in the same manner as upon money.

a. ABC Television Network
b. Interest
c. AIG
d. Insolvency

6. _____ is the state or fact of exclusive rights and control over property, which may be an object, land/real estate or intellectual property. An _____ right is also referred to as title.

_____ is the key building block in the development of the capitalist socio-economic system.

a. Encumbrance
b. Ownership
c. ABC Television Network
d. Administrative proceeding

7. A _____ is a company that owns enough voting stock in another firm to control management and operations by influencing or electing its board of directors; the second company being deemed as a subsidiary of the _____. The definition of a _____ differs from jurisdiction to jurisdiction, with the definition normally being defined by way of laws dealing with companies in that jurisdiction.

The _____-subsidiary company relationship is defined by Part 1.2, Division 6, Section 46 of the Corporations Act 2001 (Cth), which states:

Chapter 10. Consolidated Financial Statements: Special Problems

A body corporate (in this section called the first body) is a subsidiary of another body corporate if, and only if:

(a) the other body:

(i) controls the composition of the first body's board; or

(ii) is in a position to cast, or control the casting of, more than one-half of the maximum number of votes that might be cast at a general meeting of the first body; or

(iii) holds more than one-half of the issued share capital of the first body (excluding any part of that issued share capital that carries no right to participate beyond a specified amount in a distribution of either profits or capital); or

(b) the first body is a subsidiary of a subsidiary of the other body.

a. 3M Company
b. Subsidiary
c. BMC Software, Inc.
d. Parent company

8. A _____, in business matters, is an entity that is controlled by a bigger and more powerful entity. The controlled entity is called a company, corporation, or limited liability company, and the controlling entity is called its parent (or the parent company.) The reason for this distinction is that a lone company cannot be a _____ of any organization; only an entity representing a legal fiction as a separate entity can be a _____.
    a. Subsidiary
    b. 3M Company
    c. BMC Software, Inc.
    d. Parent company

9. _____ is a form of corporation equity ownership represented in the securities. It is a stock whose dividends are based on market fluctuations. It is dangerous in comparison to preferred shares and some other investment options, in that in the event of bankruptcy, _____ investors receive their funds after preferred stock holders, bondholders, creditors, etc. On the other hand, common shares on average perform better than preferred shares or bonds over time.
    a. Stock split
    b. Growth investing
    c. 3M Company
    d. Common stock

Chapter 10. Consolidated Financial Statements: Special Problems

10. _____ is typically a 'higher ranking' stock than voting shares, and its terms are negotiated between the corporation and the investor.

_____ usually carries no voting rights, but may carry superior priority over common stock in the payment of dividends and upon liquidation. _____ may carry a dividend that is paid out prior to any dividends being paid to common stock holders.

a. Cash flow
b. Restricted stock
c. Gross income
d. Preferred stock

11. _____ are payments made by a corporation to its shareholder members. It is the portion of corporate profits paid out to stockholders. When a corporation earns a profit or surplus, that money can be put to two uses: it can either be re-invested in the business (called retained earnings), or it can be paid to the shareholders as a dividend.

a. Dividend yield
b. Dividend stripping
c. Dividend payout ratio
d. Dividends

12. A _____ or reacquired stock is stock which is bought back by the issuing company, reducing the amount of outstanding stock on the open market ('open market' including insiders' holdings).

Stock repurchases are often used as a tax-efficient method to put cash into shareholders' hands, rather than pay dividends. Sometimes, companies do this when they feel that their stock is undervalued on the open market.

a. Matching principle
b. Cost of goods sold
c. Treasury stock
d. Net profit

13. _____ is a doctrine in the tax law of the United States under which a transaction must have an economic purpose aside from reduction of tax liability in order to be considered valid. This doctrine is used to determine whether tax shelters, or strategies used to reduce tax liability, are considered 'abusive' by the Internal Revenue Service.

a. ABC Television Network
b. Economic substance
c. Excise stamp
d. Occupational privilege tax

Chapter 11. International Accounting Standards; Accounting for Foreign Currency Transactions

1. The _____ is a private, not-for-profit organization whose primary purpose is to develop generally accepted accounting principles (GAAP) within the United States in the public's interest. The Securities and Exchange Commission (SEC) designated the _____ as the organization responsible for setting accounting standards for public companies in the U.S. It was created in 1973, replacing the Accounting Principles Board and the Committee on Accounting Procedure of the American Institute of Certified Public Accountants. The _____'s mission is 'to establish and improve standards of financial accounting and reporting for the guidance and education of the public, including issuers, auditors, and users of financial information.'

The _____ is not a governmental body.

a. Public company
b. Financial Accounting Standards Board
c. Governmental Accounting Standards Board
d. Fannie Mae

2. The _____ founded on April 1, 2001 is the successor of the International Accounting Standards Committee (IASC) founded in June 1973 in London. It is responsible for developing the International Financial Reporting Standards (new name for the International Accounting Standards issued after 2001), and promoting the use and application of these standards.

The _____ is an independent, privately-funded accounting standard-setter based in London, UK.

a. Information Systems Audit and Control Association
b. Emerging technologies
c. Institute of Management Accountants
d. International Accounting Standards Board

3. The U.S. _____ is an independent agency of the United States government which holds primary responsibility for enforcing the federal securities laws and regulating the securities industry, the nation's stock and options exchanges, and other electronic securities markets. The SEC was created by section 4 of the Securities Exchange Act of 1934 (now codified as 15 U.S.C. §Â§ 78d and commonly referred to as the 1934 Act.)

a. BNSF Railway
b. Securities and Exchange Commission
c. 3M Company
d. BMC Software, Inc.

4. In monetary economics _____ can refer either to a particular _____, for example British Pounds or United States Dollars, or, to the coins and banknotes of a particular _____, which actually form only a small part of the monetary base of a nation's money supply. The other part of a nation's money supply consists of money deposited in banks (sometimes called deposit money), ownership of which can be transferred by means of checks (cheques in the United Kingdom and Australia) or other forms of money transfer such as credit and debit cards. Deposit money and _____ are 'money' in the sense that both are acceptable as a means of exchange, but money need not necessarily be '_____'.

Chapter 11. International Accounting Standards; Accounting for Foreign Currency

Transactions

a. Currency
b. 3M Company
c. BNSF Railway
d. BMC Software, Inc.

5. The _____ is the national, professional association of CPAs in the United States, with more than 330,000 members, including CPAs in business and industry, public practice, government, and education; student affiliates; and international associates. It sets ethical standards for the profession and U.S. auditing standards for audits of private companies; federal, state and local governments; and non-profit organizations.

Approximately 40% of its members are engaged in the practice of public accounting, in areas such as auditing, accounting, taxation, general business consulting, business valuation, personal financial planning and business technology.

a. American Institute of Certified Public Accountants
b. AIG
c. Other postemployment benefits
d. ABC Television Network

6. An _____ is a practitioner of accountancy, which is the measurement, disclosure or provision of assurance about financial information that helps managers, investors, tax authorities and other decision makers make resource allocation decisions.

The word '_____' is derived from the French 'Compter' which took its origin from the Latin 'Computare'. The word was formerly written in English as 'Accomptant', but in process of time the word, which was always pronounced by dropping the 'p', became gradually changed both in pronunciation and in orthography to its present form.

a. Accountant
b. AIG
c. ABC Television Network
d. AMEX

7. _____ is the statutory title of qualified accountants in the United States who have passed the Uniform _____ Examination and have met additional state education and experience requirements for certification as a _____. Individuals who have passed the Exam but have not either accomplished the required on-the-job experience or have previously met it but in the meantime have lapsed their continuing professional education are, in many states, permitted the designation '_____ Inactive' or an equivalent phrase. In most U.S. states, only _____s who are licensed are able to provide to the public attestation (including auditing) opinions on financial statements.

Chapter 11. International Accounting Standards; Accounting for Foreign Currency Transactions

a. Certified General Accountant
b. Chartered Certified Accountant
c. Certified Public Accountant
d. Chartered Accountant

8. _____ are standards and interpretations adopted by the International Accounting Standards Board (IASB.)

Many of the standards forming part of _____ are known by the older name of International Accounting Standards (IAS.) IAS were issued between 1973 and 2001 by the board of the International Accounting Standards Committee (IASC.)

a. International Financial Reporting Standards
b. AIG
c. Out-of-pocket
d. ABC Television Network

9. In finance, the _____ between two currencies specifies how much one currency is worth in terms of the other. It is the value of a foreign nation's currency in terms of the home nation's currency. For example an _____ of 102 Japanese yen to the United States dollar means that JPY 102 is worth the same as USD 1.

a. ABC Television Network
b. AIG
c. Exchange rate
d. AMEX

10. The spot price or _____ of a commodity, a security or a currency is the price that is quoted for immediate (spot) settlement (payment and delivery.) Spot settlement is normally one or two business days from trade date. This is in contrast with the forward price established in a forward contract or futures contract, where contract terms (price) are set now, but delivery and payment will occur at a future date.

a. Market liquidity
b. Market price
c. Financial instruments
d. Spot rate

11. In economics, a _____, in its common usage, is a currency not backed by a national government (and not necessarily legal tender), and intended to trade only in a small area. These currencies are also referred to as community currency, or complementary currency. They encompass a wide range of forms, both physically and financially, and often are associated with a particular economic discourse.

Chapter 11. International Accounting Standards; Accounting for Foreign Currency Transactions

a. BNSF Railway
b. BMC Software, Inc.
c. 3M Company
d. Local currency

12. A _____, also client, buyer or purchaser is the buyer or user of the paid products of an individual or organization, mostly called the supplier or seller. This is typically through purchasing or renting goods or services.
a. 3M Company
b. BMC Software, Inc.
c. BNSF Railway
d. Customer

13. A _____ is the pinnacle activity involved in selling products or services in return for money or other compensation. It is an act of completion of a commercial activity.

A _____ is completed by the seller, the owner of the goods.

a. Sale
b. Maturity
c. Tertiary sector of economy
d. High yield stock

14. A _____ is a type of debt Like all debt instruments, a _____ entails the redistribution of financial assets over time, between the lender and the borrower.
a. Debenture
b. Lender
c. Loan to value
d. Loan

15. The _____ on a financial instrument is the nominal or face amount that is used to calculate payments made on that instrument. This amount generally does not change hands and is thus referred to as notional.

Chapter 11. International Accounting Standards; Accounting for Foreign Currency Transactions

Contrast a bond with an interest rate swap:

- In a bond, the buyer pays the principal amount at issue (start), then receives coupons (computed off this principal) over the life of the bond, then receives the principal back at maturity (end.)
- In a swap, no principal changes hands at inception (start) or expiry (end), and in the meantime, interest payments are computed based on a _____, which acts as if it were the principal of a bond, hence the term notional principal amount, abbreviated to notional.

a. BNSF Railway
b. 3M Company
c. Notional amount
d. BMC Software, Inc.

16. _____ is the balance of the amounts of cash being received and paid by a business during a defined period of time, sometimes tied to a specific project. Measurement of _____ can be used

- to evaluate the state or performance of a business or project.
- to determine problems with liquidity. Being profitable does not necessarily mean being liquid. A company can fail because of a shortage of cash, even while profitable.
- to project rate of returns. The time of _____s into and out of projects are used as inputs to financial models such as internal rate of return, and net present value.
- to examine income or growth of a business when it is believed that accrual accounting concepts do not represent economic realities. Alternately, _____ can be used to 'validate' the net income generated by accrual accounting.

_____ as a generic term may be used differently depending on context, and certain _____ definitions may be adapted by analysts and users for their own uses. Common terms include operating _____ and free _____.

a. Cash flow
b. Flow-through entity
c. Controlling interest
d. Commercial paper

17. A _____ is a hedge of the exposure to the variability of cash flow that

1. is attributable to a particular risk associated with a recognized asset or liability. Such as all or some future interest payments on variable rate debt or a highly probable forecast transaction and
2. could affect profit or loss

Chapter 11. International Accounting Standards; Accounting for Foreign Currency Transactions

a. Credit risk
b. 3M Company
c. Currency risk
d. Cash flow hedge

18. _____, also called fair price (in a commonplace conflation of the two distinct concepts), is a concept used in finance and economics, defined as a rational and unbiased estimate of the potential market price of a good, service, or asset, taking into account such objective factors as:

- acquisition/production/distribution costs, replacement costs, or costs of close substitutes
- actual utility at a given level of development of social productive capability
- supply vs. demand

and subjective factors such as

- risk characteristics
- cost of capital
- individually perceived utility

In accounting, _____ is used as an estimate of the market value of an asset (or liability) for which a market price cannot be determined (usually because there is no established market for the asset.) Under GAAP (FAS 157), _____ is the amount at which the asset could be bought or sold in a current transaction between willing parties, or transferred to an equivalent party, other than in a liquidation sale. This is used for assets whose carrying value is based on mark-to-market valuations; for assets carried at historical cost, the _____ of the asset is not used. One example of where _____ is an issue is a College kitchen with a cost of $2 million which was built 5 years ago.

a. BNSF Railway
b. BMC Software, Inc.
c. 3M Company
d. Fair value

Chapter 11. International Accounting Standards; Accounting for Foreign Currency Transactions

19. _____ means the giving out of information, either voluntarily or to be in compliance with legal regulations or workplace rules.

- In Computer security, full _____ means disclosing full information about vulnerabilities.
- In computing, _____ widget
- Journalism, full _____ refers to disclosing the interests of the writer which may bear on the subject being written about, for example, if the writer has worked with an interview subject in the past.

- In law:
    - The law of England and Wales, _____ refers to a process that may form part of legal proceedings, whereby parties inform to other parties the existence of any relevant documents that are, or have been, in their control. This compares with the process known as discovery in the course of legal proceedings in the United States.
    - In U.S. civil procedure (litigation rules for civil cases), _____ is a stage prior to trial. In civil cases, each party must disclose to the opposing party the following: names of witnesses which it may use to support its side, copies of documents (or mere description of these documents) in its control which it may use to support its side, computation of damages claimed, and certain insurance information. _____ is related to, but technically prior to, the discovery stage.
    - In Company law (known as 'corporate law' in the United States), _____ refers to giving out information about public or limited companies or their officers, which might be kept secret if the company was a private company or a partnership.

- In real property transactions, _____ refers to providing to a buyer information known to the seller or broker/agent concerning the condition or other aspects of real property that would affect the property's value or desirability. These rules regarding what information must be disclosed, and whether the information must be disclosed even if a buyer does not ask, vary from one jurisdiction to the next.

a. Tax harmonisation
b. Trailing
c. Disclosure
d. Controlled Foreign Corporations

20. A _____ is any one of a variety of different systems, institutions, procedures, social relations and infrastructures whereby persons trade, and goods and services are exchanged, forming part of the economy. It is an arrangement that allows buyers and sellers to exchange things. _____s vary in size, range, geographic scale, location, types and variety of human communities, as well as the types of goods and services traded.
a. Perfect competition
b. Market Failure
c. Recession
d. Market

Chapter 11. International Accounting Standards; Accounting for Foreign Currency Transactions

21. _____ is the risk that the value of an investment will decrease due to moves in market factors. The four standard _____ factors are:

- Equity risk, the risk that stock prices will change.
- Interest rate risk, the risk that interest rates will change.
- Currency risk, the risk that foreign exchange rates will change.
- Commodity risk, the risk that commodity prices (e.g. grains, metals) will change.

As with other forms of risk, _____ may be measured in a number of ways. Traditionally, this is done using a Value at Risk methodology. Value at risk is well established as a risk management technique, but it contains a number of limiting assumptions that constrain its accuracy.

a. Credit risk
b. Currency risk
c. 3M Company
d. Market risk

22. _____ is a concept that denotes the precise probability of specific eventualities. Technically, the notion of _____ is independent from the notion of value and, as such, eventualities may have both beneficial and adverse consequences. However, in general usage the convention is to focus only on potential negative impact to some characteristic of value that may arise from a future event.

a. Discount factor
b. Discounting
c. Risk adjusted return on capital
d. Risk

23. _____ are formal records of a business' financial activities.

In British English, including United Kingdom company law, _____ are often referred to as accounts, although the term _____ is also used, particularly by accountants.

_____ provide an overview of a business' financial condition in both short and long term.

a. Statement of retained earnings
b. 3M Company
c. Financial statements
d. Notes to the financial statements

24. _____ is the monetary unit of account of the principal economic environment in which an economic entity operates.

Chapter 11. International Accounting Standards; Accounting for Foreign Currency Transactions

Statement of Financial Standards No. 52 (SFAS 52) is the primary source of GAAP for translation of foreign currency financial statements.

a. 3M Company
b. BMC Software, Inc.
c. Functional currency
d. BNSF Railway

Chapter 12. Translation of Foreign Currency Financial Statements

1. The _____ is a private, not-for-profit organization whose primary purpose is to develop generally accepted accounting principles (GAAP) within the United States in the public's interest. The Securities and Exchange Commission (SEC) designated the _____ as the organization responsible for setting accounting standards for public companies in the U.S. It was created in 1973, replacing the Accounting Principles Board and the Committee on Accounting Procedure of the American Institute of Certified Public Accountants. The _____'s mission is 'to establish and improve standards of financial accounting and reporting for the guidance and education of the public, including issuers, auditors, and users of financial information.'

The _____ is not a governmental body.

   a. Governmental Accounting Standards Board
   b. Public company
   c. Fannie Mae
   d. Financial Accounting Standards Board

2. In monetary economics _____ can refer either to a particular _____, for example British Pounds or United States Dollars, or, to the coins and banknotes of a particular _____, which actually form only a small part of the monetary base of a nation's money supply. The other part of a nation's money supply consists of money deposited in banks (sometimes called deposit money), ownership of which can be transferred by means of checks (cheques in the United Kingdom and Australia) or other forms of money transfer such as credit and debit cards. Deposit money and _____ are 'money' in the sense that both are acceptable as a means of exchange, but money need not necessarily be '_____'.
   a. BNSF Railway
   b. 3M Company
   c. BMC Software, Inc.
   d. Currency

3. _____ are formal records of a business' financial activities.

In British English, including United Kingdom company law, _____ are often referred to as accounts, although the term _____ is also used, particularly by accountants.

_____ provide an overview of a business' financial condition in both short and long term.

   a. Statement of retained earnings
   b. 3M Company
   c. Notes to the financial statements
   d. Financial statements

4. _____ is the monetary unit of account of the principal economic environment in which an economic entity operates.

Chapter 12. Translation of Foreign Currency Financial Statements

Statement of Financial Standards No. 52 (SFAS 52) is the primary source of GAAP for translation of foreign currency financial statements.

a. BNSF Railway
b. Functional currency
c. BMC Software, Inc.
d. 3M Company

5. _____ is the balance of the amounts of cash being received and paid by a business during a defined period of time, sometimes tied to a specific project. Measurement of _____ can be used

- to evaluate the state or performance of a business or project.
- to determine problems with liquidity. Being profitable does not necessarily mean being liquid. A company can fail because of a shortage of cash, even while profitable.
- to project rate of returns. The time of _____s into and out of projects are used as inputs to financial models such as internal rate of return, and net present value.
- to examine income or growth of a business when it is believed that accrual accounting concepts do not represent economic realities. Alternately, _____ can be used to 'validate' the net income generated by accrual accounting.

_____ as a generic term may be used differently depending on context, and certain _____ definitions may be adapted by analysts and users for their own uses. Common terms include operating _____ and free _____.

a. Commercial paper
b. Controlling interest
c. Flow-through entity
d. Cash flow

6. In accounting, _____ has a very specific meaning. It is an outflow of cash or other valuable assets from a person or company to another person or company. This outflow of cash is generally one side of a trade for products or services that have equal or better current or future value to the buyer than to the seller.
a. AIG
b. AMEX
c. ABC Television Network
d. Expense

Chapter 12. Translation of Foreign Currency Financial Statements

7. A _____ is any one of a variety of different systems, institutions, procedures, social relations and infrastructures whereby persons trade, and goods and services are exchanged, forming part of the economy. It is an arrangement that allows buyers and sellers to exchange things. _____s vary in size, range, geographic scale, location, types and variety of human communities, as well as the types of goods and services traded.

   a. Recession
   b. Market Failure
   c. Perfect competition
   d. Market

8. _____ in economics and business is the result of an exchange and from that trade we assign a numerical monetary value to a good, service or asset. If Alice trades Bob 4 apples for an orange, the _____ of an orange is 4 apples. Inversely, the _____ of an apple is 1/4 oranges.

   a. Transactional Net Margin Method
   b. Price discrimination
   c. Discounts and allowances
   d. Price

9. A _____ is the pinnacle activity involved in selling products or services in return for money or other compensation. It is an act of completion of a commercial activity.

   A _____ is completed by the seller, the owner of the goods.

   a. Maturity
   b. Tertiary sector of economy
   c. High yield stock
   d. Sale

10. In finance, the _____ between two currencies specifies how much one currency is worth in terms of the other. It is the value of a foreign nation's currency in terms of the home nation's currency. For example an _____ of 102 Japanese yen to the United States dollar means that JPY 102 is worth the same as USD 1.

    a. ABC Television Network
    b. AMEX
    c. AIG
    d. Exchange rate

Chapter 12. Translation of Foreign Currency Financial Statements

11. A _____ is a hedge of the exposure to the variability of cash flow that

   1. is attributable to a particular risk associated with a recognized asset or liability. Such as all or some future interest payments on variable rate debt or a highly probable forecast transaction and
   2. could affect profit or loss

   a. Currency risk
   b. Cash flow hedge
   c. 3M Company
   d. Credit risk

12. An _____ is a tax levied on the financial income of people, corporations, or other legal entities. Various _____ systems exist, with varying degrees of tax incidence. Income taxation can be progressive, proportional, or regressive.
   a. Ordinary income
   b. Individual Retirement Arrangement
   c. Implied level of government service
   d. Income tax

13. The _____ founded on April 1, 2001 is the successor of the International Accounting Standards Committee (IASC) founded in June 1973 in London. It is responsible for developing the International Financial Reporting Standards (new name for the International Accounting Standards issued after 2001), and promoting the use and application of these standards.

   The _____ is an independent, privately-funded accounting standard-setter based in London, UK.

   a. Institute of Management Accountants
   b. International Accounting Standards Board
   c. Emerging technologies
   d. Information Systems Audit and Control Association

Chapter 12. Translation of Foreign Currency Financial Statements

14. _____ means the giving out of information, either voluntarily or to be in compliance with legal regulations or workplace rules.

- In Computer security, full _____ means disclosing full information about vulnerabilities.
- In computing, _____ widget
- Journalism, full _____ refers to disclosing the interests of the writer which may bear on the subject being written about, for example, if the writer has worked with an interview subject in the past.

- In law:
    - The law of England and Wales, _____ refers to a process that may form part of legal proceedings, whereby parties inform to other parties the existence of any relevant documents that are, or have been, in their control. This compares with the process known as discovery in the course of legal proceedings in the United States.
    - In U.S. civil procedure (litigation rules for civil cases), _____ is a stage prior to trial. In civil cases, each party must disclose to the opposing party the following: names of witnesses which it may use to support its side, copies of documents (or mere description of these documents) in its control which it may use to support its side, computation of damages claimed, and certain insurance information. _____ is related to, but technically prior to, the discovery stage.
    - In Company law (known as 'corporate law' in the United States), _____ refers to giving out information about public or limited companies or their officers, which might be kept secret if the company was a private company or a partnership.

- In real property transactions, _____ refers to providing to a buyer information known to the seller or broker/agent concerning the condition or other aspects of real property that would affect the property's value or desirability. These rules regarding what information must be disclosed, and whether the information must be disclosed even if a buyer does not ask, vary from one jurisdiction to the next.

a. Controlled Foreign Corporations
b. Tax harmonisation
c. Disclosure
d. Trailing

Chapter 13. Reporting for Components; Interim Reports; Reporting for the SEC

1. The _____ is a private, not-for-profit organization whose primary purpose is to develop generally accepted accounting principles (GAAP) within the United States in the public's interest. The Securities and Exchange Commission (SEC) designated the _____ as the organization responsible for setting accounting standards for public companies in the U.S. It was created in 1973, replacing the Accounting Principles Board and the Committee on Accounting Procedure of the American Institute of Certified Public Accountants. The _____'s mission is 'to establish and improve standards of financial accounting and reporting for the guidance and education of the public, including issuers, auditors, and users of financial information.'

The _____ is not a governmental body.

   a. Governmental Accounting Standards Board
   b. Fannie Mae
   c. Public company
   d. Financial Accounting Standards Board

2. The U.S. _____ is an independent agency of the United States government which holds primary responsibility for enforcing the federal securities laws and regulating the securities industry, the nation's stock and options exchanges, and other electronic securities markets. The SEC was created by section 4 of the Securities Exchange Act of 1934 (now codified as 15 U.S.C. §Â§ 78d and commonly referred to as the 1934 Act.)
   a. BMC Software, Inc.
   b. BNSF Railway
   c. 3M Company
   d. Securities and Exchange Commission

Chapter 13. Reporting for Components; Interim Reports; Reporting for the SEC

3. _____ means the giving out of information, either voluntarily or to be in compliance with legal regulations or workplace rules.

- In Computer security, full _____ means disclosing full information about vulnerabilities.
- In computing, _____ widget
- Journalism, full _____ refers to disclosing the interests of the writer which may bear on the subject being written about, for example, if the writer has worked with an interview subject in the past.

- In law:
    - The law of England and Wales, _____ refers to a process that may form part of legal proceedings, whereby parties inform to other parties the existence of any relevant documents that are, or have been, in their control. This compares with the process known as discovery in the course of legal proceedings in the United States.
    - In U.S. civil procedure (litigation rules for civil cases), _____ is a stage prior to trial. In civil cases, each party must disclose to the opposing party the following: names of witnesses which it may use to support its side, copies of documents (or mere description of these documents) in its control which it may use to support its side, computation of damages claimed, and certain insurance information. _____ is related to, but technically prior to, the discovery stage.
    - In Company law (known as 'corporate law' in the United States), _____ refers to giving out information about public or limited companies or their officers, which might be kept secret if the company was a private company or a partnership.

- In real property transactions, _____ refers to providing to a buyer information known to the seller or broker/agent concerning the condition or other aspects of real property that would affect the property's value or desirability. These rules regarding what information must be disclosed, and whether the information must be disclosed even if a buyer does not ask, vary from one jurisdiction to the next.

a. Trailing
b. Tax harmonisation
c. Controlled Foreign Corporations
d. Disclosure

4. In accounting, _____ has a very specific meaning. It is an outflow of cash or other valuable assets from a person or company to another person or company. This outflow of cash is generally one side of a trade for products or services that have equal or better current or future value to the buyer than to the seller.
  a. ABC Television Network
  b. AMEX
  c. AIG
  d. Expense

Chapter 13. Reporting for Components; Interim Reports; Reporting for the SEC

5. _____, Quarterly Report Pursuant to Section 13 or 15(d) of the Securities Exchange Act of 1934, is an SEC filing that must be filed quarterly with the US Securities and Exchange Commission. It contains similar information to the annual form 10-K, however the information is generally less detailed, and the financial statements are generally unaudited. Information for the final quarter of a firm's fiscal year is included in the 10-K, so only three 10-Q filings are made each year.
    a. Form 8-K
    b. Form 20-F
    c. 3M Company
    d. Form 10-Q

6. _____ were published by Accounting Principles Board (APB.) The board was created by American Institute of Certified Public Accountants (AICPA) in 1959 and was replaced by Financial Accounting Standards Board (FASB) in 1973. Its mission was to develop an overall conceptual framework of US generally accepted accounting principles (US GAAP.)
    a. Accounting Principles Board Opinions
    b. ABC Television Network
    c. AIG
    d. AMEX

7. _____ are formal records of a business' financial activities.

In British English, including United Kingdom company law, _____ are often referred to as accounts, although the term _____ is also used, particularly by accountants.

_____ provide an overview of a business' financial condition in both short and long term.

   a. 3M Company
   b. Financial statements
   c. Notes to the financial statements
   d. Statement of retained earnings

8. _____ is an equity (stock) exchange located at 11 Wall Street in lower Manhattan, New York, USA.) It is the largest stock exchange in the world by dollar value of its listed companies' securities. As of October 2008, the combined capitalization of all domestic _____ listed companies was US$10.1 trillion.
    a. BNSF Railway
    b. BMC Software, Inc.
    c. New York Stock Exchange
    d. 3M Company

Chapter 13. Reporting for Components; Interim Reports; Reporting for the SEC

9. A _____, (formerly a securities exchange) is a corporation or mutual organization which provides 'trading' facilities for stock brokers and traders, to trade stocks and other securities. _____s also provide facilities for the issue and redemption of securities as well as other financial instruments and capital events including the payment of income and dividends. The securities traded on a _____ include: shares issued by companies, unit trusts, derivatives, pooled investment products and bonds.
   a. BNSF Railway
   b. BMC Software, Inc.
   c. 3M Company
   d. Stock Exchange

10. _____, Gross profit margin or Gross Profit Rate can be defined as the amount of contribution to the business enterprise, after paying for direct-fixed and direct-variable unit costs, required to cover overheads (fixed commitments) and provide a buffer for unknown items. It expresses the relationship between gross profit and sales revenue.

It can be expressed in absolute terms:

Gross Profit = Revenue − Cost of Goods Sold

or as the ratio of gross profit to sales revenue, usually in the form of a percentage:

_____ Percentage = (Revenue-Cost of Goods Sold)/Revenue

Cost of goods sold includes variable costs and fixed costs directly linked to the product, such as material and labor.

   a. BNSF Railway
   b. Gross margin
   c. 3M Company
   d. BMC Software, Inc.

11. An _____ is a tax levied on the financial income of people, corporations, or other legal entities. Various _____ systems exist, with varying degrees of tax incidence. Income taxation can be progressive, proportional, or regressive.
   a. Implied level of government service
   b. Income tax
   c. Ordinary income
   d. Individual Retirement Arrangement

Chapter 13. Reporting for Components; Interim Reports; Reporting for the SEC

12. A _____ is an annual report required by the U.S. Securities and Exchange Commission (SEC), that gives a comprehensive summary of a public company's performance. Although similarly named, the annual report on _____ is distinct from the often glossy 'annual report to shareholders', which a company must send to its shareholders when it holds an annual meeting to elect directors (though some companies combine the annual report and the 10-K into one document.) The 10-K includes information such as company history, organizational structure, executive compensation, equity, subsidiaries, and audited financial statements, among other information.
    a. Form 10-K
    b. Form 10-Q
    c. 3M Company
    d. Form 8-K

13. _____ is a report required to be filed by public companies with the United States Securities and Exchange Commission pursuant to the Securities Exchange Act of 1934, as amended. After a significant event like bankruptcy or departure of a CEO, a public company generally must file a Current Report on _____ within four business days to provide an update to previously filed quarterly reports on Form 10-Q and/or Annual Reports on Form 10-K. _____ is a very broad form used to notify investors of any unscheduled material event that is important to shareholders or the SEC.
    a. Form 20-F
    b. 3M Company
    c. Form 10-Q
    d. Form 8-K

14. An _____ is a legal contract between two parties, particularly for indentured labour or a term of apprenticeship but also for certain land transactions. The term comes from the medieval English '_____ of retainer' -- a legal contract written in duplicate on the same sheet, with the copies separated by cutting along a jagged line so that the teeth of the two parts could later be refitted to confirm authenticity. Each party to the deed would then retain a part.
    a. Impracticability
    b. Operating Lease
    c. Employee Retirement Income Security Act
    d. Indenture

15. The _____, codified at 15 U.S.C. § 80b-1 through 15 U.S.C. § 80b-21, is a United States federal law that was created to regulate the actions of investment advisers (also spelled 'advisors') as defined by the law.
    a. Investment Advisers Act of 1940
    b. Express warranty
    c. Exclusive right
    d. Independent contractor

Chapter 13. Reporting for Components; Interim Reports; Reporting for the SEC

16. An _____ is a company whose main business is holding securities of other companies purely for investment purposes. The _____ invests money on behalf of its shareholders who in turn share in the profits and losses.

In United States securities law, there are at least three types of investment companies :

- Open-End Management Investment Companies (mutual funds)
- Closed-End Management Investment Companies (closed-end funds)
- UITs (unit investment trusts)

A fourth and lesser-known type of _____ under the _____ Act of 1940 is a Face-Amount Certificate Company.

a. AIG
b. Investment Company
c. AMEX
d. ABC Television Network

17. The _____ is an act of Congress. It was passed as a United States Public Law (PL-768) on August 22, 1940, and is codified at 15 U.S.C. Â§ 80a-1 through 15 U.S.C.
a. AMEX
b. AIG
c. Investment Company Act of 1940
d. ABC Television Network

18. The term _____ usually refers to a company that is permitted to offer its registered securities (stock, bonds, etc.) for sale to the general public, typically through a stock exchange, or occasionally a company whose stock is traded over the counter (OTC) via market makers who use non-exchange quotation services.

The term '_____' may also refer to a company owned by the government.

a. Professional association
b. MicroStrategy
c. Governmental Accounting Standards Board
d. Public Company

19. The _____ (sometimes called 'Peekaboo') is a private-sector, non-profit corporation created by the Sarbanes-Oxley Act, a 2002 United States federal law, to oversee the auditors of public companies. Its stated purpose is to 'protect the interests of investors and further the public interest in the preparation of informative, fair, and independent audit reports'. Although a private entity, the _____ has many government-like regulatory functions, making it in some ways similar to the private Self Regulatory Organizations (SROs) that regulate stock markets and other aspects of the financial markets in the United States.
   a. Pension Benefit Guaranty Corporation
   b. 3M Company
   c. Financial Crimes Enforcement Network
   d. Public Company Accounting Oversight Board

20. A _____ is a fungible, negotiable instrument representing financial value. they are broadly categorized into debt securities (such as banknotes, bonds and debentures), and equity securities; e.g., common stocks. The company or other entity issuing the _____ is called the issuer.
   a. Tracking stock
   b. BMC Software, Inc.
   c. Security
   d. 3M Company

21. Congress enacted the _____, in the aftermath of the stock market crash of 1929 and during the ensuing Great Depression.
   a. Securities Act of 1933
   b. Sustainability measurement
   c. Bookkeeping
   d. Monte Carlo methods

22. The _____ of 1934 is a law governing the secondary trading of securities (stocks, bonds, and debentures) in the United States of America. The Act, 48 Stat. 881 (enacted June 6, 1934), codified at 15 U.S.C.
   a. BMC Software, Inc.
   b. Securities Exchange Act
   c. BNSF Railway
   d. 3M Company

23. The _____ is a law governing the secondary trading of securities (stocks, bonds, and debentures) in the United States of America. The Act, 48 Stat. 881 (enacted June 6, 1934), codified at 15 U.S.C.

Chapter 13. Reporting for Components; Interim Reports; Reporting for the SEC 69

a. 3M Company
b. Securities Exchange Act of 1934
c. BNSF Railway
d. BMC Software, Inc.

24. The United States _____ Act of 1939 (Trust indentureA), codified at 15 U.S.C. Â§ 77aaa through 15 U.S.C. Â§ 77bbbb, supplements the Securities Act of 1933 in the case of the distribution of debt securities.
   a. Robinson-Patman Act
   b. Charter
   c. Covenant
   d. Trust Indenture

25. The United States _____, codified at 15 U.S.C. Â§ 77aaa through 15 U.S.C. Â§ 77bbbb, supplements the Securities Act of 1933 in the case of the distribution of debt securities.
   a. Coming into force
   b. Burden of proof
   c. Lease
   d. Trust Indenture Act of 1939

26. _____ are financial statements that factor the holding company's subsidiaries into its aggregated accounting figure. It is a representation of how the holding company is doing as a group. The consolidated accounts should provide a true and fair view of the financial and operating conditions of the group.
   a. Consolidated financial statements
   b. Redemption value
   c. Replacement cost
   d. Committee on Accounting Procedure

27. _____ is a fee paid on borrowed assets. It is the price paid for the use of borrowed money, or, money earned by deposited funds. Assets that are sometimes lent with _____ include money, shares, consumer goods through hire purchase, major assets such as aircraft, and even entire factories in finance lease arrangements. The _____ is calculated upon the value of the assets in the same manner as upon money.
   a. Insolvency
   b. ABC Television Network
   c. Interest
   d. AIG

Chapter 13. Reporting for Components; Interim Reports; Reporting for the SEC

28. _____ is the state or fact of exclusive rights and control over property, which may be an object, land/real estate or intellectual property. An _____ right is also referred to as title.

_____ is the key building block in the development of the capitalist socio-economic system.

a. Ownership
b. Encumbrance
c. ABC Television Network
d. Administrative proceeding

29. A _____, in business matters, is an entity that is controlled by a bigger and more powerful entity. The controlled entity is called a company, corporation, or limited liability company, and the controlling entity is called its parent (or the parent company.) The reason for this distinction is that a lone company cannot be a _____ of any organization; only an entity representing a legal fiction as a separate entity can be a _____.

a. Parent company
b. BMC Software, Inc.
c. 3M Company
d. Subsidiary

Chapter 14. Bankruptcy: Liquidation and Reorganization

1. _____ means the inability to pay one's debts as they fall due. Usually used in Business terms, _____ refers to the inability for a 'limited liability' company to pay off debts.

This is defined in two different ways:

Cash flow _____ -
    Unable to pay debts as they fall due.

  a. Insolvency
  b. Interest
  c. AIG
  d. ABC Television Network

2. An _____ is a term used in behavioral economics to describe those types of behaviors that impose costs on a person in the long-run that are not taken into account when making decisions in the present. Classical Economics discourages government from creating legislation that targets internalities, because it is assumed that the consumer takes these personal costs into account when paying for the good that causes the _____. For example, cigarettes should be taxed because of the negative consumption externalities that they impose, such as second-hand smoke, not because the smoker harms him or herself by smoking.
  a. Inventory turnover ratio
  b. Authorised capital
  c. Operating budget
  d. Internality

3. The _____ is the United States federal government agency that collects taxes and enforces the internal revenue laws. It is an agency within the U.S. Dept of the treasury responsible for interpretation and application of Federal tax law. The official U.S. Treasury regulations provide (in part):

The _____ is a bureau of the Department of the Treasury under the immediate direction of the Commissioner of Internal Revenue.

  a. Use tax
  b. Indirect tax
  c. Income tax
  d. Internal Revenue Service

Chapter 14. Bankruptcy: Liquidation and Reorganization

4. _____ is a legally declared inability or impairment of ability of an individual or organization to pay its creditors. Creditors may file a _____ petition against a debtor ('involuntary _____') in an effort to recoup a portion of what they are owed or initiate a restructuring. In the majority of cases, however, _____ is initiated by the debtor (a 'voluntary _____' that is filed by the bankrupt individual or organization.)
   a. Bankruptcy protection
   b. 3M Company
   c. BMC Software, Inc.
   d. Bankruptcy

5. In law, _____ refers to the process by which a company (or part of a company) is brought to an end, and the assets and property of the company redistributed. _____ can also be referred to as winding-up or dissolution, although dissolution technically refers to the last stage of _____. The process of _____ also arises when customs, an authority or agency in a country responsible for collecting and safeguarding customs duties, determines the final computation or ascertainment of the duties or drawback accruing on an entry.
   a. BMC Software, Inc.
   b. Liquidation
   c. Bankruptcy protection
   d. 3M Company

6. A _____ is a fungible, negotiable instrument representing financial value. they are broadly categorized into debt securities (such as banknotes, bonds and debentures), and equity securities; e.g., common stocks. The company or other entity issuing the _____ is called the issuer.
   a. BMC Software, Inc.
   b. Security
   c. Tracking stock
   d. 3M Company

7. A _____ is a party (e.g. person, organization, company, or government) that has a claim to the services of a second party. It is a person or institution to whom money is owed. The first party, in general, has provided some property or service to the second party under the assumption (usually enforced by contract) that the second party will return an equivalent property or service.
   a. Payback period
   b. Treasury company
   c. Par value
   d. Creditor

8. In economics a _____ is an entity that owes a debt to someone else. The entity may be an individual, a firm, a government, a company or other legal person. The counterparty is called a creditor.

Chapter 14. Bankruptcy: Liquidation and Reorganization

a. Segregated portfolio company
b. Fair market value
c. Debtor
d. Shares authorized

9. _____ is any physical or virtual entity that is owned by an individual or jointly by a group of individuals. An owner of _____ has the right to consume, sell, rent, mortgage, transfer and exchange his or her _____. Important widely-recognized types of _____ include real _____, personal _____ (other physical possessions), and intellectual _____ (rights over artistic creations, inventions, etc.), although the latter is not always as widely recognized or enforced.

a. Disclosure requirement
b. Fiduciary
c. Primary authority
d. Property

10. _____ is a legal term that refers to a holder of property on behalf of a beneficiary. A trust can be set up either to benefit particular persons, or for any charitable purposes (but not generally for non-charitable purposes): typical examples are a will trust for the testator's children and family, a pension trust (to confer benefits on employees and their families), and a charitable trust. In all cases, the _____ may be a person or company, whether or not they are a prospective beneficiary.

a. Cash cow
b. Performance measurement
c. Management by exception
d. Trustee

11. _____ are financial statements that factor the holding company's subsidiaries into its aggregated accounting figure. It is a representation of how the holding company is doing as a group. The consolidated accounts should provide a true and fair view of the financial and operating conditions of the group.

a. Replacement cost
b. Committee on Accounting Procedure
c. Consolidated financial statements
d. Redemption value

12. A _____ is a business that functions without the intention or threat of liquidation for the foreseeable future, usually regarded as at least within 12 months.

In accounting, '_____' refers to a company's ability to continue functioning as a business entity. It is the responsibility of the directors to assess whether the _____ assumption is appropriate when preparing the financial statements.

a. 3M Company
b. BMC Software, Inc.
c. Payment
d. Going concern

13. _____ are journal entries made at the end of an accounting period to transfer temporary accounts to permanent accounts. An 'income summary' account may be used to show the balance between revenue and expenses, or they could be directly closed against retained earnings where dividend payments will be deducted from. This process is used to reset the balance of these temporary accounts to zero for the next accounting period.
   a. Closing entries
   b. Treasury stock
   c. Trial balance
   d. FIFO and LIFO accounting

14. In monetary economics _____ can refer either to a particular _____, for example British Pounds or United States Dollars, or, to the coins and banknotes of a particular _____, which actually form only a small part of the monetary base of a nation's money supply. The other part of a nation's money supply consists of money deposited in banks (sometimes called deposit money), ownership of which can be transferred by means of checks (cheques in the United Kingdom and Australia) or other forms of money transfer such as credit and debit cards. Deposit money and _____ are 'money' in the sense that both are acceptable as a means of exchange, but money need not necessarily be '_____'.
   a. BMC Software, Inc.
   b. BNSF Railway
   c. 3M Company
   d. Currency

15. _____ are formal records of a business' financial activities.

In British English, including United Kingdom company law, _____ are often referred to as accounts, although the term _____ is also used, particularly by accountants.

_____ provide an overview of a business' financial condition in both short and long term.

   a. 3M Company
   b. Notes to the financial statements
   c. Statement of retained earnings
   d. Financial statements

Chapter 14. Bankruptcy: Liquidation and Reorganization

16. _____ means the giving out of information, either voluntarily or to be in compliance with legal regulations or workplace rules.

- In Computer security, full _____ means disclosing full information about vulnerabilities.
- In computing, _____ widget
- Journalism, full _____ refers to disclosing the interests of the writer which may bear on the subject being written about, for example, if the writer has worked with an interview subject in the past.

- In law:
    - The law of England and Wales, _____ refers to a process that may form part of legal proceedings, whereby parties inform to other parties the existence of any relevant documents that are, or have been, in their control. This compares with the process known as discovery in the course of legal proceedings in the United States.
    - In U.S. civil procedure (litigation rules for civil cases), _____ is a stage prior to trial. In civil cases, each party must disclose to the opposing party the following: names of witnesses which it may use to support its side, copies of documents (or mere description of these documents) in its control which it may use to support its side, computation of damages claimed, and certain insurance information. _____ is related to, but technically prior to, the discovery stage.
    - In Company law (known as 'corporate law' in the United States), _____ refers to giving out information about public or limited companies or their officers, which might be kept secret if the company was a private company or a partnership.

- In real property transactions, _____ refers to providing to a buyer information known to the seller or broker/agent concerning the condition or other aspects of real property that would affect the property's value or desirability. These rules regarding what information must be disclosed, and whether the information must be disclosed even if a buyer does not ask, vary from one jurisdiction to the next.

a. Trailing
b. Tax harmonisation
c. Controlled Foreign Corporations
d. Disclosure

Chapter 15. Estates and Trusts

1. A _____ is a party (e.g. person, organization, company, or government) that has a claim to the services of a second party. It is a person or institution to whom money is owed. The first party, in general, has provided some property or service to the second party under the assumption (usually enforced by contract) that the second party will return an equivalent property or service.
    a. Par value
    b. Payback period
    c. Treasury company
    d. Creditor

2. _____ is a legal term that refers to a holder of property on behalf of a beneficiary. A trust can be set up either to benefit particular persons, or for any charitable purposes (but not generally for non-charitable purposes): typical examples are a will trust for the testator's children and family, a pension trust (to confer benefits on employees and their families), and a charitable trust. In all cases, the _____ may be a person or company, whether or not they are a prospective beneficiary.
    a. Trustee
    b. Performance measurement
    c. Cash cow
    d. Management by exception

Chapter 16. Nonprofit Organizations

1. The general definition of an _____ is an evaluation of a person, organization, system, process, project or product. _____s are performed to ascertain the validity and reliability of information; also to provide an assessment of a system's internal control. The goal of an _____ is to express an opinion on the person/organization/system (etc) in question, under evaluation based on work done on a test basis.

   a. Institute of Chartered Accountants of India
   b. Audit regime
   c. Audit
   d. Assurance service

2. The _____ is a private, not-for-profit organization whose primary purpose is to develop generally accepted accounting principles (GAAP) within the United States in the public's interest. The Securities and Exchange Commission (SEC) designated the _____ as the organization responsible for setting accounting standards for public companies in the U.S. It was created in 1973, replacing the Accounting Principles Board and the Committee on Accounting Procedure of the American Institute of Certified Public Accountants. The _____'s mission is 'to establish and improve standards of financial accounting and reporting for the guidance and education of the public, including issuers, auditors, and users of financial information.'

   The _____ is not a governmental body.

   a. Financial Accounting Standards Board
   b. Fannie Mae
   c. Governmental Accounting Standards Board
   d. Public company

3. _____ is an accounting system often used by nonprofit organizations and by the public sector. According to StartHereGoPlaces, _____ is a '[m]ethod of accounting and presentation whereby assets and liabilities are grouped according to the purpose for which they are to be used.'

   _____ serves any nonprofit organization or the public sector. These organizations have a need for special reporting to financial statements users that show how money is spent, rather than how much profit was earned.

   a. Liquidating dividend
   b. Replacement cost
   c. Refunding
   d. Fund accounting

4. A _____ is a body of elected or appointed members who jointly oversee the activities of a company or organization. The body sometimes has a different name, such as board of trustees, board of governors, board of managers, or executive board. It is often simply referred to as 'the board.'

Chapter 16. Nonprofit Organizations

A board's activities are determined by the powers, duties, and responsibilities delegated to it or conferred on it by an authority outside itself.

a. Chief Financial Officers Act of 1990
b. Hospital Survey and Construction Act
c. Consumer protection laws
d. Board of directors

5. Project _____: The project _____ is a prediction of the costs associated with a particular company project. These costs include labor, materials, and other related expenses. The project _____ is often broken down into specific tasks, with task _____s assigned to each.

a. BNSF Railway
b. BMC Software, Inc.
c. 3M Company
d. Budget

6. An _____ is a tax levied on the financial income of people, corporations, or other legal entities. Various _____ systems exist, with varying degrees of tax incidence. Income taxation can be progressive, proportional, or regressive.

a. Individual Retirement Arrangement
b. Implied level of government service
c. Ordinary income
d. Income tax

7. In accounting, _____ has a very specific meaning. It is an outflow of cash or other valuable assets from a person or company to another person or company. This outflow of cash is generally one side of a trade for products or services that have equal or better current or future value to the buyer than to the seller.

a. AIG
b. ABC Television Network
c. AMEX
d. Expense

8. The term _____ is used in finance theory to refer to any terminating stream of fixed payments over a specified period of time. This usage is most commonly seen in academic discussions of finance, usually in connection with the valuation of the stream of payments, taking into account time value of money concepts such as interest rate and future value.

Examples of these are regular deposits to a savings account, monthly home mortgage payments and monthly insurance payments.

a. Annuity
b. Appropriation
c. Intangible
d. Improvement

9. _____ are financial statements that factor the holding company's subsidiaries into its aggregated accounting figure. It is a representation of how the holding company is doing as a group. The consolidated accounts should provide a true and fair view of the financial and operating conditions of the group.
   a. Redemption value
   b. Consolidated financial statements
   c. Replacement cost
   d. Committee on Accounting Procedure

10. _____ are journal entries made at the end of an accounting period to transfer temporary accounts to permanent accounts. An 'income summary' account may be used to show the balance between revenue and expenses, or they could be directly closed against retained earnings where dividend payments will be deducted from. This process is used to reset the balance of these temporary accounts to zero for the next accounting period.
    a. FIFO and LIFO accounting
    b. Trial balance
    c. Treasury stock
    d. Closing entries

11. In monetary economics _____ can refer either to a particular _____, for example British Pounds or United States Dollars, or, to the coins and banknotes of a particular _____, which actually form only a small part of the monetary base of a nation's money supply. The other part of a nation's money supply consists of money deposited in banks (sometimes called deposit money), ownership of which can be transferred by means of checks (cheques in the United Kingdom and Australia) or other forms of money transfer such as credit and debit cards. Deposit money and _____ are 'money' in the sense that both are acceptable as a means of exchange, but money need not necessarily be '_____'.
    a. BMC Software, Inc.
    b. BNSF Railway
    c. 3M Company
    d. Currency

12. _____ are formal records of a business' financial activities.

In British English, including United Kingdom company law, _____ are often referred to as accounts, although the term _____ is also used, particularly by accountants.

_____ provide an overview of a business' financial condition in both short and long term.

a. Financial statements
b. 3M Company
c. Notes to the financial statements
d. Statement of retained earnings

13. A _____ is a type of debt Like all debt instruments, a _____ entails the redistribution of financial assets over time, between the lender and the borrower.
 a. Debenture
 b. Loan to value
 c. Lender
 d. Loan

Chapter 17. Governmental Entities: General Fund

1. The _____ is currently the source of generally accepted accounting principles (GAAP) used by State and Local governments in the [[United States of America]]. As with most of the entities involved in creating GAAP in the United States, it is a private, non-governmental organization.

   The _____ is subject to oversight by the Financial Accounting Foundation (FAF), which selects the members of the _____ and the Financial Accounting Standards Board, and funds both organizations.

   a. Fannie Mae
   b. Governmental Accounting Standards Board
   c. National Conference of Commissioners on Uniform State Laws
   d. Multinational corporation

2. _____ is an umbrella term which refers to the various accounting systems used by various public sector entities. In the United States, for instance, there are two levels of government which follow different accounting standards set forth by independent, private sector boards. At the federal level, the Federal Accounting Standards Advisory Board (FASAB) sets forth the accounting standards to follow.
   a. Nonassurance services
   b. Product control
   c. Governmental Accounting
   d. Management accounting

3. _____ is an accounting system often used by nonprofit organizations and by the public sector. According to StartHereGoPlaces, _____ is a '[m]ethod of accounting and presentation whereby assets and liabilities are grouped according to the purpose for which they are to be used.'

   _____ serves any nonprofit organization or the public sector. These organizations have a need for special reporting to financial statements users that show how money is spent, rather than how much profit was earned.

   a. Liquidating dividend
   b. Replacement cost
   c. Refunding
   d. Fund accounting

4. In economics, _____ or _____ goods or real _____ refers to factors of production used to create goods or services that are not themselves significantly consumed (though they may depreciate) in the production process. _____ goods may be acquired with money or financial _____. In finance and accounting, _____ generally refers to financial wealth, especially that used to start or maintain a business.

a. Vyborg Appeal
b. Capital
c. Screening
d. Disclosure

5. _____ is that which is owed; usually referencing assets owed, but the term can also cover moral obligations and other interactions not requiring money. In the case of assets, _____ is a means of using future purchasing power in the present before a summation has been earned. Some companies and corporations use _____ as a part of their overall corporate finance strategy.
   a. Debenture
   b. Lender
   c. Loan
   d. Debt

6. An _____ is a term used in behavioral economics to describe those types of behaviors that impose costs on a person in the long-run that are not taken into account when making decisions in the present. Classical Economics discourages government from creating legislation that targets internalities, because it is assumed that the consumer takes these personal costs into account when paying for the good that causes the _____. For example, cigarettes should be taxed because of the negative consumption externalities that they impose, such as second-hand smoke, not because the smoker harms him or herself by smoking.
   a. Inventory turnover ratio
   b. Operating budget
   c. Authorised capital
   d. Internality

7. The term _____ or superannuation refers to a pension granted upon retirement. They may be set up by employers, insurance companies, the government or other institutions such as employer associations or trade unions.
   a. BMC Software, Inc.
   b. 3M Company
   c. Retirement plan
   d. Wage

8. The word _____ indicates that a party, or proprietor, exercises private ownership, control or use over an item of property

Chapter 17. Governmental Entities: General Fund

a. BMC Software, Inc.
b. 3M Company
c. BNSF Railway
d. Proprietary

9. _____ are formal records of a business' financial activities.

In British English, including United Kingdom company law, _____ are often referred to as accounts, although the term _____ is also used, particularly by accountants.

_____ provide an overview of a business' financial condition in both short and long term.

a. Financial statements
b. 3M Company
c. Notes to the financial statements
d. Statement of retained earnings

10. Project _____: The project _____ is a prediction of the costs associated with a particular company project. These costs include labor, materials, and other related expenses. The project _____ is often broken down into specific tasks, with task _____s assigned to each.
a. BMC Software, Inc.
b. BNSF Railway
c. Budget
d. 3M Company

11. _____ of something is, in finance, the adding together of interest or different investments over a period of time such as atoms (1 - the act or process of accruing; 2 - the amount that accrues.) It holds specific meanings in accounting and payroll.

_____, in accounting, describes the accounting method known as _____ basis, whereby revenues and expenses are recognized when they are accrued, i.e. accumulated (earned or incurred), regardless when the actual cash is received or paid out.

a. Accrual
b. Accounts receivable
c. Assets
d. Earnings before interest, taxes, depreciation and amortization

Chapter 17. Governmental Entities: General Fund

12. _____ is a method of accounting whereby economic activities (rather than cash flow) of financial events are considered, because of two complementary principles, which (together) determine the point, at which expenses and revenues are recognized. According to revenue recognition principle, revenues are realized when earned, whether or not they are received in cash.

   a. Earnings before interest, taxes, depreciation and amortization
   b. Accrued revenue
   c. Accrual
   d. Accrual basis accounting

13. _____ is a legal term of art for anything that affects or limits the title of a property, such as mortgages, leases, easements, liens, or restrictions. Also, those considered as potentially making the title defeasible are also _____s. For example, charging orders, building orders and structure alteration.

   a. Administrative proceeding
   b. ABC Television Network
   c. Ownership
   d. Encumbrance

Chapter 18. Governmental Entities: Other Governmental Funds and Account Groups 85

1. _____ is an accounting system often used by nonprofit organizations and by the public sector. According to StartHereGoPlaces, _____ is a '[m]ethod of accounting and presentation whereby assets and liabilities are grouped according to the purpose for which they are to be used.'

_____ serves any nonprofit organization or the public sector. These organizations have a need for special reporting to financial statements users that show how money is spent, rather than how much profit was earned.

  a. Replacement cost
  b. Liquidating dividend
  c. Refunding
  d. Fund accounting

2. The U.S. _____ is an independent agency of the United States government which holds primary responsibility for enforcing the federal securities laws and regulating the securities industry, the nation's stock and options exchanges, and other electronic securities markets. The SEC was created by section 4 of the Securities Exchange Act of 1934 (now codified as 15 U.S.C. ÂÂ§ 78d and commonly referred to as the 1934 Act.)
  a. BMC Software, Inc.
  b. 3M Company
  c. BNSF Railway
  d. Securities and Exchange Commission

3. _____ are formal records of a business' financial activities.

In British English, including United Kingdom company law, _____ are often referred to as accounts, although the term _____ is also used, particularly by accountants.

_____ provide an overview of a business' financial condition in both short and long term.

  a. Statement of retained earnings
  b. Notes to the financial statements
  c. 3M Company
  d. Financial statements

4. In economics, _____ or _____ goods or real _____ refers to factors of production used to create goods or services that are not themselves significantly consumed (though they may depreciate) in the production process. _____ goods may be acquired with money or financial _____. In finance and accounting, _____ generally refers to financial wealth, especially that used to start or maintain a business.

Chapter 18. Governmental Entities: Other Governmental Funds and Account Groups

   a. Vyborg Appeal
   b. Screening
   c. Capital
   d. Disclosure

5. In finance, a _____ is a debt security, in which the authorized issuer owes the holders a debt and, depending on the terms of the _____, is obliged to pay interest (the coupon) and/or to repay the principal at a later date, termed maturity. It is a formal contract to repay borrowed money with interest at fixed intervals.

Thus a _____ is like a loan: the issuer is the borrower, the _____ holder is the lender, and the coupon is the interest.

   a. Zero-coupon bond
   b. Revenue bonds
   c. Coupon rate
   d. Bond

6. _____ is that which is owed; usually referencing assets owed, but the term can also cover moral obligations and other interactions not requiring money. In the case of assets, _____ is a means of using future purchasing power in the present before a summation has been earned. Some companies and corporations use _____ as a part of their overall corporate finance strategy.
   a. Loan
   b. Debenture
   c. Lender
   d. Debt

7. The _____ is currently the source of generally accepted accounting principles (GAAP) used by State and Local governments in the [[United States of America]]. As with most of the entities involved in creating GAAP in the United States, it is a private, non-governmental organization.

The _____ is subject to oversight by the Financial Accounting Foundation (FAF), which selects the members of the _____ and the Financial Accounting Standards Board, and funds both organizations.

   a. Fannie Mae
   b. National Conference of Commissioners on Uniform State Laws
   c. Governmental Accounting Standards Board
   d. Multinational corporation

Chapter 18. Governmental Entities: Other Governmental Funds and Account Groups 87

8. In business and accounting, _____ are everything of value that is owned by a person or company. It is a claim on the property your income of a borrower. The balance sheet of a firm records the monetary value of the _____ owned by the firm.
   a. Accounts receivable
   b. Earnings before interest, taxes, depreciation and amortization
   c. Assets
   d. Accrual basis accounting

9. The term _____ has three unrelated technical definitions, and is also used in a variety of non-technical ways.

   - In financial economics, it refers to any asset used to make money, as opposed to assets used for personal enjoyment or consumption. This is an important distinction because two people can disagree sharply about the value of personal assets, one person might think a sports car is more valuable than a pickup truck, another person might have the opposite taste. But if an asset is held for the purpose of making money, taste has nothing to do with it, only differences of opinion about how much money the asset will produce. With the further assumption that people agree on the probability distribution of future cash flows, it is possible to have an objective _____ pricing model. Even without the assumption of agreement, it is possible to set rational limits on _____ value.
   - In governmental accounting, it is defined as any asset used in operations with an initial useful life extending beyond one reporting period. Generally, government managers have a 'stewardship' duty to maintain _____ s under their control. See International Public Sector Accounting Standards for details.
   - In US tax accounting, it is defined as any property other than a list of exceptions. The main exceptions are anything held for sale, and any real estate or depreciable property used in business. Almost everything you own and use for personal purposes, pleasure or investment is a _____. If something is a _____ for tax purposes, gains or losses on sale or disposition are capital gains or capital losses. For individuals, however, capital losses on property held for personal use are generally not deductible. See the IRS publication Tax Facts about Capital Gains and Losses for details.

A well-known financial accounting textbook advises that the term be avoided except in tax accounting because it is used in so many different senses, not all of them well-defined. For example it is often used as a synonym for fixed assets or for investments in securities.

A common non-technical usage occurs when people ask that employees or the environment or something else be treated as a _____.

   a. Solvency
   b. Capital asset
   c. 3M Company
   d. BMC Software, Inc.

Chapter 18. Governmental Entities: Other Governmental Funds and Account Groups

10. In economic models, the _____ time frame assumes no fixed factors of production. Firms can enter or leave the marketplace, and the cost (and availability) of land, labor, raw materials, and capital goods can be assumed to vary. In contrast, in the short-run time frame, certain factors are assumed to be fixed, because there is not sufficient time for them to change.
    a. Short-run
    b. BMC Software, Inc.
    c. Long-run
    d. 3M Company

11. _____ is a type of lease - the other being an operating lease. A _____ effectively allows a firm to finance the purchase of an asset, even if, strictly speaking, the firm never acquires the asset. Typically, a _____ will give the lessee control over an asset for a large proportion of the asset's useful life, providing them the benefits and risks of ownership.
    a. Profitability index
    b. Finance lease
    c. Debt ratio
    d. 3M Company

12. The _____ is a private, not-for-profit organization whose primary purpose is to develop generally accepted accounting principles (GAAP) within the United States in the public's interest. The Securities and Exchange Commission (SEC) designated the _____ as the organization responsible for setting accounting standards for public companies in the U.S. It was created in 1973, replacing the Accounting Principles Board and the Committee on Accounting Procedure of the American Institute of Certified Public Accountants. The _____'s mission is 'to establish and improve standards of financial accounting and reporting for the guidance and education of the public, including issuers, auditors, and users of financial information.'

    The _____ is not a governmental body.

    a. Fannie Mae
    b. Governmental Accounting Standards Board
    c. Public company
    d. Financial Accounting Standards Board

13. A _____ is a contract conferring a right on one person to possess property belonging to another person (called a landlord or lessor) to the exclusion of the owner landlord. It is a rental agreement between landlord and tenant. The relationship between the tenant and the landlord is called a tenancy, and the right to possession by the tenant is sometimes called a leasehold interest.

a. Federal Sentencing Guidelines
b. Model Code of Professional Responsibility
c. Robinson-Patman Act
d. Lease

Chapter 19. Governmental Entities: Proprietary Funds, Fiduciary Funds, Annual Report

1. _____ is an accounting system often used by nonprofit organizations and by the public sector. According to StartHereGoPlaces, _____ is a '[m]ethod of accounting and presentation whereby assets and liabilities are grouped according to the purpose for which they are to be used.'

_____ serves any nonprofit organization or the public sector. These organizations have a need for special reporting to financial statements users that show how money is spent, rather than how much profit was earned.

   a. Replacement cost
   b. Refunding
   c. Liquidating dividend
   d. Fund accounting

2. An _____ is a term used in behavioral economics to describe those types of behaviors that impose costs on a person in the long-run that are not taken into account when making decisions in the present. Classical Economics discourages government from creating legislation that targets internalities, because it is assumed that the consumer takes these personal costs into account when paying for the good that causes the _____. For example, cigarettes should be taxed because of the negative consumption externalities that they impose, such as second-hand smoke, not because the smoker harms him or herself by smoking.

   a. Internality
   b. Inventory turnover ratio
   c. Operating budget
   d. Authorised capital

3. The word _____ indicates that a party, or proprietor, exercises private ownership, control or use over an item of property

   a. BNSF Railway
   b. BMC Software, Inc.
   c. 3M Company
   d. Proprietary

4. _____ are formal records of a business' financial activities.

In British English, including United Kingdom company law, _____ are often referred to as accounts, although the term _____ is also used, particularly by accountants.

_____ provide an overview of a business' financial condition in both short and long term.

Chapter 19. Governmental Entities: Proprietary Funds, Fiduciary Funds, Annual Report

a. Statement of retained earnings
b. 3M Company
c. Notes to the financial statements
d. Financial statements

5. The _____ is currently the source of generally accepted accounting principles (GAAP) used by State and Local governments in the [[United States of America]]. As with most of the entities involved in creating GAAP in the United States, it is a private, non-governmental organization.

The _____ is subject to oversight by the Financial Accounting Foundation (FAF), which selects the members of the _____ and the Financial Accounting Standards Board, and funds both organizations.

a. Governmental Accounting Standards Board
b. Fannie Mae
c. National Conference of Commissioners on Uniform State Laws
d. Multinational corporation

6. The _____ duty is a legal relationship of confidence or trust between two or more parties, most commonly a _____ or trustee and a principal or beneficiary. One party, for example a corporate trust company or the trust department of a bank, holds a _____ relation or acts in a _____ capacity to another, such as one whose funds are entrusted to it for investment. In a _____ relation one person justifiably reposes confidence, good faith, reliance and trust in another whose aid, advice or protection is sought in some matter.
a. Staple right
b. Robinson-Patman Act
c. FCPA
d. Fiduciary

7. The _____ (sometimes called 'Peekaboo') is a private-sector, non-profit corporation created by the Sarbanes-Oxley Act, a 2002 United States federal law, to oversee the auditors of public companies. Its stated purpose is to 'protect the interests of investors and further the public interest in the preparation of informative, fair, and independent audit reports'. Although a private entity, the _____ has many government-like regulatory functions, making it in some ways similar to the private Self Regulatory Organizations (SROs) that regulate stock markets and other aspects of the financial markets in the United States.
a. Financial Crimes Enforcement Network
b. Public Company Accounting Oversight Board
c. 3M Company
d. Pension Benefit Guaranty Corporation

8. The U.S. _____ is an independent agency of the United States government which holds primary responsibility for enforcing the federal securities laws and regulating the securities industry, the nation's stock and options exchanges, and other electronic securities markets. The SEC was created by section 4 of the Securities Exchange Act of 1934 (now codified as 15 U.S.C. ÂÂ§ 78d and commonly referred to as the 1934 Act.)

   a. BMC Software, Inc.
   b. 3M Company
   c. BNSF Railway
   d. Securities and Exchange Commission

ANSWER KEY

Chapter 1
1. d   2. c   3. d   4. d   5. d   6. b   7. d   8. b   9. b   10. d
11. c   12. d   13. a   14. c   15. d   16. d   17. a   18. c   19. d

Chapter 2
1. d   2. d   3. d   4. b   5. b   6. d   7. d   8. d   9. d   10. d
11. d   12. a   13. d   14. a   15. a   16. d   17. d   18. d   19. d   20. d
21. c   22. d

Chapter 3
1. d   2. d   3. d   4. c   5. c   6. a   7. a   8. b   9. d   10. d
11. a   12. b   13. c   14. d   15. d   16. b   17. d   18. d   19. d   20. a
21. d   22. b   23. b   24. a

Chapter 4
1. d   2. c   3. d   4. d   5. c   6. d   7. b   8. d   9. d   10. a
11. d

Chapter 5
1. c   2. d   3. c   4. d   5. b   6. b   7. d   8. a   9. c   10. d
11. a   12. d

Chapter 6
1. d   2. a   3. a   4. c   5. d   6. d   7. c   8. d   9. d   10. d
11. b   12. c   13. c   14. d

Chapter 7
1. b   2. d   3. d   4. b   5. d

Chapter 8
1. d   2. c   3. a   4. d   5. b   6. b   7. d   8. b   9. d   10. a
11. d   12. d

Chapter 9
1. d   2. d   3. c   4. d   5. d   6. d   7. d   8. a   9. b   10. c
11. a   12. d   13. b   14. d   15. d

Chapter 10
1. d   2. d   3. d   4. c   5. b   6. b   7. d   8. a   9. d   10. d
11. d   12. c   13. b

Chapter 11
1. b   2. d   3. b   4. a   5. a   6. a   7. c   8. a   9. c   10. d
11. d   12. d   13. a   14. d   15. c   16. a   17. d   18. d   19. c   20. d
21. d   22. d   23. c   24. c

Chapter 12
1. d 2. d 3. d 4. b 5. d 6. d 7. d 8. d 9. d 10. d
11. b 12. d 13. b 14. c

Chapter 13
1. d 2. d 3. d 4. d 5. d 6. a 7. b 8. c 9. d 10. b
11. b 12. a 13. d 14. d 15. a 16. b 17. c 18. d 19. d 20. c
21. a 22. b 23. b 24. d 25. d 26. a 27. c 28. a 29. d

Chapter 14
1. a 2. d 3. d 4. d 5. b 6. b 7. d 8. c 9. d 10. d
11. c 12. d 13. a 14. d 15. d 16. d

Chapter 15
1. d 2. a

Chapter 16
1. c 2. a 3. d 4. d 5. d 6. d 7. d 8. a 9. b 10. d
11. d 12. a 13. d

Chapter 17
1. b 2. c 3. d 4. b 5. d 6. d 7. c 8. d 9. a 10. c
11. a 12. d 13. d

Chapter 18
1. d 2. d 3. d 4. c 5. d 6. d 7. c 8. c 9. b 10. c
11. b 12. d 13. d

Chapter 19
1. d 2. a 3. d 4. d 5. a 6. d 7. b 8. d

www.ingramcontent.com/pod-product-compliance
Lightning Source LLC
Chambersburg PA
CBHW081846230426
43669CB00018B/2844